The Sayings of CONFUCIUS

The Sayings of CONFUCIUS

BARNES
&NOBLE
BOOKS
NEW YORK

This edition published by Barnes & Noble, Inc.

1994 Barnes & Noble Books

ISBN 1-56619-228-5 *casebound*
ISBN 1-56619-227-7 *gift edition*

Book design by James Sarfati

Printed and bound in the United States of America

MG 9 8 7 6 5 4
MG 9 8 7 6 5 4 3 2

⚔ C O N T E N T S ⚔

⚔ v

◅ I N T R O D U C T I O N ▻

The name Confucius is the latinized form of the Chinese characters, K´ung Foo-tsze, meaning "The master, K´ung." The bearer of this name was born of an ancient and distinguished family in the district of Tsow, in the present province of Shen tung, China, B. C. 551. His father was a soldier of reputation and governor of Tsow, but not a man of wealth. Confucius married at nineteen, and in his early manhood held a minor office; but within a few years he became a public teacher, and soon attracted numerous disciples. Rising in reputation, he was invited to the court of Chow, where he investigated the traditional ceremonies and maxims of the ruling dynasty; and in the following year visited another state where he studied the ancient music. When he was nearly fifty, in the year 500 B. C., he again took office, becoming in turn chief magistrate of the town of Chung-too, Assistant-Superintendent of Works to the Ruler of Loo, and finally Minister of Crime. In spite of almost miraculous efficiency, he lost the support of his ruler in

496 B. C.; and until his death in 478 B. C., he wandered from state to state, sometimes well-treated, sometimes enduring severe hardships, always saddened by the refusal of the turbulent potentates to be guided by his beneficent counsels. No sooner was he dead, however, than his wisdom was recognized by peasant and emperor alike; admiration rose to veneration, veneration to worship. Sacrifices were offered to him, temples built in his honor, and a cult established which has lasted almost two thousand years.

Confucius did not regard himself as an innovator, but as the conservator of ancient truth and ceremonial propriety. He dealt with neither theology nor metaphysics, but with moral and political conduct.

The Lun Yu, Analects or Sayings of Confucius, were probably compiled, says Legge, "by the disciples of the disciples of the sage, making free use of the written memorials concerning him which they had received, and the oral statements which they had heard, from their several masters. And we shall not be far wrong, if we determine its date as about the beginning of the third, or the end of the fourth century before Christ."

1 THE MASTER SAID: "In learning and straightway practising is there not pleasure also? When friends gather round from afar do we not rejoice? Whom lack of fame cannot vex is not he a gentleman?"

2 Yu-tzu[1] said: "A dutiful son and brother is seldom fond of thwarting those over him: a man unwilling to thwart those over him is never given to crime. A gentleman nurses the roots: when the root has taken, the truth will grow; and what are the roots of love, but the duty of son and of brother?"

3 The Master said: "Honeyed words and flattering looks seldom speak of love."

[1]Disciples.

4 Tseng-tzu[1] said: "Thrice daily I ask myself: 'Have I been unfaithful in dealing for others? Have I been untrue to friends? Do I practise what I preach?'"

5 The Master said: "To guide a land of a thousand chariots, honour business, be true and sparing, love the people, and time thy claims upon them."

6 The Master said: "The young should be dutiful at home, modest abroad, heedful and true, full of goodwill for the many, close friends with love; and should they have strength to spare, let them spend it upon the arts."

7 Tzu-hsia[1] said: "If a man honour worth and forsake lust, serve father and mother with all his strength, be ready to give his life for the king, and keep faith with his friends; though men may call him rude, I call him learned."

8 The Master said: "Of a gentleman who is frivolous none stand in awe, nor can his learning be sound. Make faithfulness and truth thy masters: have no friends unlike thyself: be not ashamed to mend thy faults."

9 Tseng-tzu[1] said: "Respect death and recall forefathers, the good in men will again grow sturdy."

[1]Disciples.

10 Tzu-ch'in[1] said to Tzu-kung[1]: "The Master, on coming to a country, learns all about the government: does he ask, or is it told him?"

Tzu-kung said: "The Master learns it by his warmth and honesty, by politeness, modesty, and yielding. The way that the Master asks is unlike other men's asking."

11 The Master said: "As long as his father lives a son should study his wishes; after he is dead, he should study his life. If for three years he do not forsake his father's ways, he may be called dutiful."

12 Yu-tzu[1] said: "In daily courtesy ease is of price. This was the beauty of the old kings' ways; this they followed in small and great. But knowing this, it is not right to give way to ease, unchecked by courtesy. This also is wrong."

13 Yu-tzu said: "If promises hug the right, word can be kept: if attentions are bounded by courtesy, shame will be banished: heroes may be worshipped, if we choose them aright."

14 The Master said: "A gentleman who is not a greedy eater, nor a lover of ease at home, who is earnest in deed and careful of speech who seeks the righteous and profits by them, may be called fond of learning."

[1]Disciples.

15 Tzu-kung said: "Poor, but no flatterer; rich, but not proud. How were that?"

"Good," said the Master; "but better still were poor, yet merry; rich, yet courteous."

Tzu-kung said: "Where the poem says:

> 'If ye cut, if ye file,
> If ye polish and grind';

is that what is meant?"

The Master said: "Now I can talk of poetry to thee, Tz'u. Given a clue, thou canst find the way."

16 The Master said: "Not to be known should not grieve you: grieve that ye know not men."

1   THE MASTER SAID: "In governing, cleave to good; as the north star holds his place, and the multitude of stars revolve upon him."

2   The Master said: "To sum up, the three hundred songs in a word, they are free from evil thought."

3   The Master said: "Guide the people by law, subdue them by punishment; they may shun crime, but will be void of shame. Guide them by example, subdue them by courtesy; they will learn shame, and come to be good."

4   The Master said: "At fifteen, I was bent on study; at thirty, I could stand; at forty, doubts ceased; at fifty, I understood the laws of Heaven; at sixty, my ears obeyed me; at seventy, I could do as my heart lusted, and never swerve from right."

5 Meng Yi asked the duty of a son.

The Master said: "Obedience."

As Fan Ch´ih[1] was driving him, the Master said: "Mengsun[2] asked me the duty of a son; I answered 'Obedience.'"

"What did ye mean?" said Fan Ch´ih.

"To serve our parents with courtesy whilst they live," said the Master; "to bury them with all courtesy when they die; and to worship them with all courtesy."

6 Meng Wu asked the duty of a son.

The Master said: "What weighs on your father and mother is concern for your health."

8 Tzu-yu[3] asked the duty of a son.

The Master said: "To-day a man is called dutiful if he keep his father and mother. But we keep both our dogs and horses, and unless we honour parents, is it not all one?"

8 Tzu-hsia asked the duty of a son.

The Master said: "Our manner is the hard part. For the young to be a stay in toil, and leave the wine and cakes to their elders, is this to fulfil their duty?"

[1]A disciple.
[2]Meng Yi.
[3]A disciple.

9 The Master said: "If I talk all day to Hui,[4] like a dullard, he never stops me. But when he is gone, if I pry into his life, I find he can do what I say. No, Hui is no dullard."

10 The Master said: "Look at a man's acts; watch his motives; find out what pleases him: can the man evade you? Can the man evade you?"

11 The Master said: "Who keeps the old akindle and adds new knowledge is fitted to be a teacher."

12 The Master said: "A gentleman is not a vessel."

13 Tzu-kung asked, What is a gentleman?

The Master said: "He puts words into deed first, and sorts what he says to the deed."

14 The Master said: "A gentleman is broad and fair: the vulgar are biassed and petty."

15 The Master said: "Study without thought is vain: thought without study is dangerous."

16 The Master said: "Work on strange doctrines does harm."

17 The Master said: "Yu,[5] shall I teach thee what is understanding? To know what we know, and know what we do not know, that is understanding."

4The Master's favourite disciple, Yen Yüan.
5The disciple, Tzu-lu.

18 Tzu-chang[6] studied with an eye to pay.

The Master said: "Listen much, keep silent when in doubt, and always take heed of the tongue; thou wilt make few mistakes. See much, beware of pitfalls, and always give heed to thy walk; thou wilt have little to rue. If thy words are seldom wrong, thy deeds leave little to rue, pay will follow."

19 Duke Ai[7] asked: "What should be done to make the people loyal?"

Confucius answered: "Exalt the straight, set aside the crooked, the people will be loyal. Exalt the crooked, set aside the straight, the people will be disloyal."

20 Chi K'ang[8] asked how to make the people lowly, faithful, and willing.

The Master said: "Behave with dignity, they will be lowly: be pious and merciful, they will be faithful: exalt the good, teach the unskilful, they will grow willing."

21 One said to Confucius: "Why are ye not in power, Sir?"

The Master answered: "What does the book say of a good son? 'An always dutiful son, who is a friend to his brothers, showeth the way to rule.' This also is to rule. What need to be in power?"

6A disciple.
7Duke of Lu, during Confucius' closing years.
8Head of the Chi clan during Confucius' closing years.

22 The Master said: "Without truth I know not how man can live. A cart without a crosspole, a carriage without harness, how could they be moved?"

23 Tzu-chang asked whether we can know what is to be ten generations hence.

The Master said: "The Yin[9] inherited the manners of the Hsia;[9] the harm and the good that they wrought them is known. The Chou[9] inherited the manners of the Yin; the harm and the good that they wrought them is known. And we may know what is to be, even an hundred generations hence, when others follow Chou."

24 The Master said: "To worship the ghosts of strangers is fawning. To see the right and not do it is want of courage."

---

[9]The three dynasties that had ruled China up till the time of Confucius.

1   OF THE CHI having eight rows of dancers[1] in his hall, Confucius said: "If this is to be borne, what is not to be borne?"

2   At the end of worship, the Three Clans made use of the Yung hymn.[1]

The Master said:

> "'The dukes and princes assist,
>   Solemn is the Son of Heaven;'

what sense has this in the hall of the Three Clans?"

3   The Master said: "A man without love, what is courtesy to him? A man without love, what is music to him?"

---

[1]An imperial prerogative.

4 Lin Fang asked, What is the life of ceremony?

The Master said: "A great question! At hightides, waste is worse than thrift: at burials, grief outweighs nicety."

5 The Master said: "The wild tribes have kings; whilst the realm of Hsia[2] is without!"

6 The Chi worshipped on Mount T´ai.[3]

The Master said to Jan Yu[4]: "Canst thou not stop this?"

He answered: "I cannot."

"Alas!" said the Master; "dost thou set Mount T´ai below Lin Fang?"

7 The Master said: "A gentleman has no rivalries—except perhaps in archery; and then, as bowing he joins the winners, or steps down to see the loser drink, throughout the struggle he is still the gentleman."

8 Tzu-hsia asked: "What is the meaning of:

> 'Her cunning smiles,
> Her dimples light,
> Her lovely eyes,
> So clear and bright,
> The ground, not yet
> With colours dight'?'

[2]China.
[3]A prerogative of the Duke of Lu.
[4]A disciple, in the service of the Chi.

The Master said: "Colouring follows groundwork."

"Then does courtesy follow after?" said Tzu-hsia.

"Shang,"[5] said the Master, "thou hast hit my meaning! Now I can talk of poetry to thee."

9 The Master said: "I can speak of the manners of Hsia; but for Chi witnesses fail. I can speak of the manners of Yin; but for Sung witnesses fail. This is due to their dearth of books and great men. Were there enough of these, they would witness for me."

10 The Master said: "After the drink offering at the Great Sacrifice, I have no wish to see more."

11 One asked about the words of the Great Sacrifice.

The Master said: "I do not understand them. Could one understand them, he would overlook the world as I this"—and he pointed to his palm.

12 Worship as though those ye worship stood before you; worship the spirits, as though they stood before you.

The Master said: "If I take no part in the sacrifice, it is none to me."

[5]Tzu-hsia.

13 Wang-sun Chia[6] said: "What is the meaning of 'it is better to court the Kitchen God than the God of the Home'?"

"Not at all," said the Master. "A sin against Heaven is past praying for."

14 The Master said: "Two lines of kings have passed beneath the ken of Chou. How rich in art is Chou! It is Chou I follow."

15 On entering the Great Temple, the Master asked how each thing was done.

One said: "Who says that the man of Tsou's son has a knowledge of ceremony? On entering the Great Temple, he asked how each thing was done!"

On hearing this, the Master said: "Such is the ceremony."

16 The Master said: "To pierce through the target does not score in archery; because men differ in strength. This was the old rule."

17 Tzu-kung wished to do away with the sheep offering at the new moon.

The Master said: "Thou lovest the sheep, Tz´u: I love the rite."

---

[6]Wang-sun Chia was minister of Wei, and more influential than his master. The Kitchen God is less honourable than the God of the Home (the Roman lares), but since he sees all that goes on in the house, and ascends to Heaven at the end of the year to report what has happened, it is well to be on good terms with him.

18 The Master said: "Treat the king with all courtesy, men call it fawning."

19 Duke Ting asked how a king should behave to his ministers; how ministers should serve their king?

Confucius answered: "A king should behave with courtesy to his ministers; ministers should serve their king faithfully."

20 The Master said: "The poem 'The Osprey' is glad, but not wanton; it is sad, but not morbid."

21 Duke Ai asked Tsai Wo[7] about the shrines of the guardian spirits.

Tsai Wo answered: "The Hsia Emperors grew firs round them; the men of Yin grew cypress; the men of Chou grew chestnut, meaning '*jest not* over holy matters.'"[8]

On hearing this, the Master said: "I do not speak of what is ended, chide what is settled, or find fault with what is past."

22 The Master said: "How shallow was Kuan Chung!"[9]

"But," said one, "was not Kuan Chung thrifty?"

[7] A disciple of Confucius.
[8] *Literally* "to cause the people to be in awe." The commentators are more than usually learned over the Master's anger. I attribute it to the foolishness of the pun, and translate accordingly.
[9] Kuan Chung (+B.C. 645), a famous man in his day, was chief minister to the Duke of Ch'i, whom he raised to such wealth and power, that he became the leading prince of the empire. His chief merit lay in crushing the barbarous frontier tribes. The rest of his work, being founded in the sand, died with him.

"Kuan owned San Kuei, and in his household none doubled offices," said the Master; "was that thrift?"

"At least Kuan Chung was versed in courtesy."

The Master said: "Kings screen their gates with trees; Kuan, too, had trees to screen his gate. When two kings make merry together, they have a stand for the turned-down cups; Kuan had a turned-down cup-stand too! If Kuan were versed in courtesy, who is not versed in courtesy?"

23 The Master said to the chief musician of Lu: "How to play music may be known. At first each part in unison; then, a swell of harmony, each part distinct, rolling on to the finish."

24 The warden of Yi asked to see Confucius, saying: "No gentleman has ever come here, whom I have failed to see."

The followers presented him.

On leaving he said: "My lads, why lament your fall? The world has long been astray. Heaven will make of the Master a warning bell."

25 The Master said: "All beautiful and noble is the music of Shao! The music of Wu is as beautiful, but less noble."

26 The Master said: "Rank without bounty; ritual without reverence; mourning without grief, why should I cast them a glance?"

1   THE MASTER SAID: "Love makes a spot beautiful: who chooses not to dwell in love, has he got wisdom?"

2   The Master said: "Loveless men cannot bear need long, they cannot bear fortune long. Loving hearts find peace in love; clever heads find profit in it."

3   The Master said: "Love can alone love others, or hate others."

4   The Master said: "A heart set on love will do no wrong."

5   The Master said: "Wealth and honours are what men desire; but abide not in them by help of wrong. Lowliness and want are hated of men; but forsake them not by help of wrong.

"Shorn of love, is a gentleman worthy the name? Not for one moment may a gentleman sin against love; not in flurry and haste, nor yet in utter overthrow."

6 The Master said: "A friend to love, a foe to evil, I have yet to meet. A friend to love will set nothing higher. In love's service, a foe to evil will let no evil touch him. Were a man to give himself to love, but for one day, I have seen no one whose strength would fail him. Such men there may be, but I have not seen one."

7 The Master said: "A man and his faults are of a piece. By watching his faults we learn whether love be his."

8 The Master said: "To learn the truth at daybreak and die at eve were enough."

9 The Master said: "A scholar in search of truth who is ashamed of poor clothes and poor food it is idle talking to."

10 The Master said: "A gentleman has no likes and no dislikes below heaven. He follows right."

11 The Master said: "Gentlemen cherish worth; the vulgar cherish dirt. Gentlemen trust in justice; the vulgar trust in favour."

12 The Master said: "The chase of gain is rich in hate."

13 The Master said: "What is it to sway a kingdom by courteous yielding? Who cannot be courteous yielding sway a kingdom, what can he know of courtesy?"

14 The Master said: "Be not concerned at want of place; be concerned that thou stand thyself. Sorrow not at being unknown, but seek to be worthy of note."

15 The Master said: "One thread, Shen,[1] runs through all my teaching."

"Yes," said Tseng-tzu.

After the Master had left, the disciples asked what was meant.

Tseng-tzu said: "The Master's teaching all hangs on faithfulness and fellow-feeling."

16 The Master said: "A gentleman considers what is right; the vulgar consider what will pay."

17 The Master said: "At sight of worth, think to grow like it. When evil meets thee, search thine own heart."

18 The Master said: "A father or mother may be gently chidden. If they will not bend, be the more lowly, but persevere; nor murmur if trouble follow."

[1]The disciple Tseng-tzu.

19 The Master said: "Whilst thy father and mother live, do not wander afar. If thou must travel, hold a set course."

20 The Master said: "If for three years a son do not forsake his father's ways, he may be called dutiful."

21 The Master said: "A father's and a mother's age must be borne in mind; with joy on the one hand, fear on the other."

22 The Master said: "Men of old were loth to speak; lest a word that they could not make good should shame them."

23 The Master said: "Who contains himself goes seldom wrong."

24 The Master said: "A gentleman wishes to be slow to speak and quick to act."

25 The Master said: "Good is no hermit. It has ever neighbours."

26 Tzu-yu said: "Preaching to princes brings disgrace, nagging at friends estrangement."

1   OF KUNG-YEH CH'ANG the Master said: "A girl might marry him. In him was no crime, though he has been in bonds."

He gave him his daughter to wife.

Of Nan Jung the Master said: "When right prevails, he will not be neglected: when wrong prevails, he will escape law and punishment."

He gave him his brother's daughter to wife.

2   Of Tzu-chien[1] the Master said: "What a gentleman he is! But could he have grown to be a man like this were there no gentlemen in Lu?"

[1]A disciple, born in Lu.

3   Tzu-kung asked: "And what of me?"

"Thou art a vessel," said the Master.

"What kind of vessel?"

"A rich temple vessel."

4   "Yung,"[2] said one, "has love, but he has not a glib tongue."

The Master said: "What is the good of a glib tongue? Fighting men with tongue-craft breeds much bitterness. Whether love be his I do not know, but what is the good of a glib tongue?"

5   The Master moved Ch'i-tiao K'ai[3] to take office.

He answered: "For this I lack confidence."

The Master was pleased.

6   The Master said: "Truth makes no way. Let me go afloat and scour the sea! and Yu[4] shall follow me."

When Tzu-lu heard this he was glad.

The Master said: "Yu is more venturesome than I, but he does not know how to take things."

---

[2]The disciple Chung-kung.
[3]A disciple.
[4]The disciple Tzu-lu.

7 Meng Wu asked whether Tzu-lu had love?

The Master said: "I do not know."

He asked again.

The Master said: "A land of a thousand chariots might give Yu charge of its levies; but whether he have love, I do not know."

"And how about Ch´iu?"[5]

"A town of a thousand households, a clan of an hundred chariots might make Ch´iu governor; but whether he have love, I do not know."

"And how about Ch´ih?"[6]

"Girt with his sash, erect in the court, Ch´ih might entertain the guests; but whether he have love, I do not know."

8 The Master said to Tzu-kung: "Who is abler, thou or Hui?"[7]

He answered, "How dare I aspire to Hui? If he hear one thing, Hui understands ten; when I hear one thing, I understand two."

The Master said: "Thou art not his peer. I grant, thou art not his peer."

[5]The disciple Jan Yu.
[6]The disciple Kung-hsi Hua.
[7]The disciple Yen Yüan.

23

9 Tsai Yü[8] slept in the daytime.

The Master said: "Rotten wood cannot be carved, nor are dung walls plastered. Why chide with Yü?"

The Master said: "In my first dealings with men, I hearkened to their words, and took their deeds on trust. Now, in dealing with men, I hearken to their words, and watch their deeds. I righted this on Yü."

10 The Master said: "I have met no firm man."

One answered. "Shen Ch´ang."

The Master said: "Ch´ang is passionate: how can he be firm?"

11 Tzu-kung said: "What I do not wish to have done unto me, I likewise wish not to do unto others."

The Master said: "That is still beyond thee, Tz´u."

12 Tzu-kung said: "We may listen to the Master's culture; but on life and the ways of Heaven his words are denied us."

13 Until Tzu-lu could carry out what he heard, he only dreaded to hear more.

---

[8]The disciple Tsai Wo.

14 Tzu-kung asked: "Why was K'ung-wen styled cultured?"

The Master said: "He was quick and fond of learning, not ashamed to ask those beneath him. That is why he was called cultured."

15 Of Tzu-ch'an the Master said: "In four ways he was a gentleman. His own life was modest; he honoured the man whom he served; he was kind in rearing the people; he was just in his calls upon them."

16 The Master said: "Yen P'ing was versed in friendship. Familiarity bred courtesy."

17 The Master said: "Tsang Wen lodged his tortoise with hills on the pillars, reeds on the uprights. Was this his good sense?"

18 Tzu chang said: "Tzu wen was thrice made minister without show of gladness, and thrice left office with unmoved face. He was careful to unfold his rule to the new minister. What do ye think of him?"

"He was faithful," said the Master.

"But had he love?"

"I do not know," said the Master: "how should this amount to love?"

"When Ts'ui slew the King of Ch'i, Ch'en Wen forsook ten teams of horses, and left the land. On coming to another kingdom, he said, 'Like my lord Ts´ui,' and left it. On coming to a second kingdom, he said, 'Like my lord Ts´ui,' and left it. What do ye think of him?"

"He was pure," said the Master.

"But had he love?"

"I do not know," said the Master: "how should this amount to love?"

19 Chi Wen thought thrice before acting.

On hearing this, the Master said: "Twice, that is enough."

20 The Master said: "Whilst peace reigned in the land Ning Wu[9] showed understanding: when troubles came he turned simpleton. His understanding is within our reach; such simplicity is beyond our reach."

21 When he was in Ch´en the Master said: "Home, I must go home! My batch of boys, ambitious and hasty, their minds cultured, their schooling ended, know not what needs fashioning!"

---

[9]Ning Wu was minister to the Duke of Wei, in the middle of the seventh century B.C. The duke was driven from his throne, and deserted by the wise and prudent; but Ning Wu, in his simplicity, followed his master everywhere, and finally effected his restoration.

22 The Master said: "As Po-yi[10] and Shu-ch'i never recalled past wickedness the foes they made were few."

23 The Master said: "Who would call Wei-sheng Kao straight? A man begged him for vinegar. He begged it from a neighbour and gave it."

24 The Master said: "Honeyed words, flattering looks and overdone humility, Tso Ch'iu-ming thought shameful, and so do I. To hide ill-will and ape friendship, Tso Ch'iu-ming thought shameful, and so do I."

25 As Yen Yüan and Chi-lu[11] were sitting with him, the Master said: "Why not each of you tell me his wishes?"

Tzu-lu said: "Carriages and horses I would have, and robes of fine fur to share with my friends, and would wear them out all free from care."

Yen Yüan said: "To make no boast of talent, nor show of merit, were my wish."

Tzu-lu said: "We should like to hear your wishes, Sir."

---

[10]Po-yi and Shu-ch'i were sons of the King of Ku-chu. Their father left the throne to the younger of the two; but he would not supplant the elder, nor would the elder act against his father's wishes. So they both retired into obscurity. When King Wu overthrew the tyrant Chou (B.C. 1122), rather than live under a new dynasty, they starved to death.
[11]Tzu-lu.

The Master said: "To make the old folk happy, to be true to friends, to have a heart for the young."

26 The Master said: "It is finished! I have met no one who can see his own faults, and arraign himself within."

27 The Master said: "In a hamlet of ten households there must be men faithful and true as I: why is there no one as fond of learning?"

1 THE MASTER SAID: "Yung[1] might fill the seat of a prince."

"And might Tzu-sang Po-tzu?" asked Chung-kung.

"Yes," said the Master: "but he is lax."

"To be lax in his claims on the people might be right," said Chung-kung, "were he stern to self; but to be lax to self and lax to others must surely be over-lax."

The Master said: "What Yung says is true."

[1] The disciple Chung-kung.

2   Duke Ai asked which disciples were fond of learning.

Confucius answered: "Yen Hui[2] loved learning. His anger fell not astray; he made no mistake twice. By ill-luck his life was cut short. Now that he is gone, I hear of no one who is fond of learning."

3   Tzu-hua[3] having been sent to Ch´i, the disciple Jan asked for grain to give to his mother.

The Master said: "Give her a bushel."

He asked for more.

The Master said: "Give her half a quarter."

Jan gave her twenty-five quarters.

The Master said: "On his way to Ch´i, Ch´ih[4] was drawn by sleek horses, clad in fine furs. A gentleman, I have heard, helps the needy: he does not swell riches."

When Yüan Ssu[5] was governor his pay was nine hundred measures of grain. On his refusing it, the Master said: "Not so. Why not take it and give it to thy neighbours and country-folk?"

4   Of Chung-kung the Master said: "If the calf of a brindled cow be red and horned, though men be shy to offer him, will the hills and streams disdain him?"

[2]The disciple Yen Yüan.
[3]The disciple Kung-hsi Hua, or Kung-hsi Ch´ih.
[4]The disciple Kung-hsi Hua, or Kung-hsi Ch´ih.
[5]A disciple.

5 The Master said: "For three months together Hui's[6] heart never sinned against love. The others may hold out for a day, or a month; but no more."

6 Chi K'ang[7] asked whether Chung-yu[8] were fit for power.

The Master said: "Yu[8] has character; what would governing be to him?"

"And Tz'u,[9] is he fit for power?"

"Tz'u is intelligent; what would governing be to him?"

"And Ch'iu,[10] is he fit for power?"

"Ch'iu has ability; what would governing be to him?"

7 The Chi sent to make Min Tzu-ch'ien[11] governor of Pi.

Min Tzu-ch'ien said: "Make some good excuse for me. If he send again, I must be across the Wen."

8 When Po-niu[11] was ill the Master went to ask after him. Grasping his hand through the window, he said: "He is dying. It is our lot. But why this man of such an illness? why this man of such an illness?"

---

[6] The disciple Yen Yüan.
[7] Head of the Chi clan after the death of Chi Huan.
[8] The disciple Tzu-lu.
[9] The disciple Tzu-kung.
[10] The disciple Jan Yu.
[11] Disciples.

9 The Master said: "What a man was Hui![12] A dish of rice, a gourd of water, in a low alleyway; no man can bear such misery! Yet Hui never fell from mirth. What a man he was!"

10 Jan Ch´iu[13] said: "Pleasure in the Master's path I do not lack: I lack strength."

The Master said: "Who lacks strength faints by the way; thou puttest a curb upon thee."

11 The Master said to Tzu-hsia: "Read to become a gentleman; do not read as the vulgar do."

12 When Tzu-yu was governor of Wu-ch´eng,[14] the Master said: "Hast thou gotten any men?"

He answered: "I have Tan-t´ai Mieh-ming. When walking he will not take a short-cut; he has never come to my house except on business."

13 The Master said: "Meng Chih-fan never bragged. He was covering the rear in a rout; but when the gate was reached, he whipped up his horse and cried: 'Not courage kept me behind; my horse won't go!'"

---

[12]The disciple Yen Yüan.
[13]The disciple Jan Yu.
[14]A town in Lu, belonging to the Chi.

14 The Master said: "Unless glib as the reader T'o, and handsome as Chao of Sung, escape is hard in the times that be!"

15 The Master said: "Who can go out except by the door? Why is it no one keeps to the way?"

16 The Master said: "Nature outweighing art begets roughness; art outweighing nature begets pedantry. Art and nature well blent make a gentleman."

17 The Master said: "Man is born upright. If he cease to be so and live, he is lucky to escape!"

18 The Master said: "Who knows does not rank with him who likes, nor he who likes with him who is glad therein."

19 The Master said: "To men above the common we may speak of things above the common. To men below the common we must not speak of things above the common."

20 Fan Ch'ih[15] asked, What is wisdom?

The Master said: "To foster right amongst the people; to honour the ghosts of the dead, whilst keeping aloof from them, may be called wisdom."

He asked, What is love?

The Master said: "To rank the effort above the prize may be called love."

[15] A disciple.

21 The Master said: "Wisdom delights in water; love delights in hills. Wisdom is stirring; love is quiet. Wisdom enjoys life; love grows old."

22 The Master said: "By one revolution Ch´i might grow as Lu: by one revolution Lu might win to truth."

23 The Master said: "A drinking horn that is no horn! What a horn! What a drinking horn!"

24 Tsai Wo[16] said: "Were a man who loves told that there is a man in a well, would he go after him?" The Master said: Why should he? A gentleman might be brought to the well, but not entrapped into it. He may be cheated; he is not to be fooled."

25 The Master said: "By breadth of reading and the ties of courtesy a gentleman will also keep from error's path."

26 The Master saw Nan-tzu.[17] Tzu-lu was displeased. The Master took an oath, saying: "If there were sin in me may Heaven forsake me, may Heaven forsake me!"

27 The Master said: "The highest goodness is to hold fast the golden mean. Amongst the people it has long been rare."

---

[16] A disciple.
[17] The dissolute wife of Duke Ling of Wei.

28 Tzu-kung said: "To treat the people with bounty and help the many, how were that? Could it be called love?"

The Master said: "What has this to do with love? Would it not be holiness? Both Yao and Shun[18] still yearned for this. In seeking a foothold for self, love finds a foothold for others; seeking light for itself, it enlightens others also. To learn from the near at hand may be called the key to love."

---

[18]Two emperors of the golden age.

1   THE MASTER SAID: "A teller and not a maker, one who trusts and loves the past; I may be likened to our old P'eng."[1]

2   The Master said: "A silent communer, an ever hungry learner, a still unflagging teacher; am I any of these?"

3   The Master said: "Neglect of what is good in me; want of thoroughness in study; failure to do the right when told me; lack of strength to overcome faults, these are my sorrows."

4   In his free moments the Master was easy and cheerful.

[1]Of old P'eng we should be glad to know more, but "the rest is silence."

5 The Master said: "How deep is my decay! It is long since I saw the Duke of Chou[2] in a dream."

6 The Master said: "Will the right; hold to good won; rest in love; move in art."

7 The Master said: "From the man who paid in dried meat upwards, I have withheld teaching from no one."

8 The Master said: "Only to those fumbling do I open, only for those stammering do I find the word. From him who cannot turn the whole when I lift a corner I desist."

9 When eating beside a mourner the Master never ate his fill. On days when he had been wailing, the Master did not sing.

10 The Master said to Yen Yüan: "I and thou alone can both fill a post when given one and live unseen when passed by."

Tzu-lu said: "Had ye to command three armies, Sir, who should go with you?"

"No man," said the Master, "ready to fly unarmed at a tiger, or plunge into a river and die without a pang should be with me; but one, rather, who is wary before a move and gains his end by well-laid plans."

---

[2]Died B.C. 1105. He was the younger brother of King Wu, the founder of the Chou dynasty, as great in peace as the king in war.

11 The Master said: "Were shouldering a whip a sure road to riches, I would turn carter: but since there is no sure road, I tread the path I love."

12 The Master gave heed to devotions, war, and sickness.

13 When the Master was in Ch´i for three months after hearing the Shao played he knew not the taste of meat.

"I did not suppose," he said, "that music could touch such heights."

14 Jan Yu said: "Is the Master for the King of Wei?"[3]

"I will ask him," said Tzu-kung.

He went in, and said: "What kind of men were Po-yi[4] and Shu-ch´i?"

"Worthy men of yore," said the Master.

"Did they rue the past?"

"They sought love and found it; what had they to rue?"

Tzu-kung went out, and said: "The Master is not on his side."

---

[3]The grandson of Duke Ling, husband of Nan-tzu. His father had been driven from the country for planning to kill Nantzu. When Duke Ling died, he was succeeded by his grandson, who opposed by force his father's attempts to seize the throne.
[4]See note to 5.22.

15 The Master said: "Living on coarse rice and water, with bent arm for pillow, mirth may be ours; but ill-gotten wealth and honours are to me a wandering cloud."

16 The Master said: "Given a few more years, making fifty for the study of the Yi,[5] I might be purged from gross sin."

17 The Master liked to talk of poetry, history, and the upkeep of courtesy. Of all these he was fond of talking.

18 The Duke of She asked Tzu-lu about Confucius.

Tzu-lu did not answer.

The Master said: "Why couldst thou not say: 'He is a man so eager that he forgets to eat, whose cares are lost in triumph, unmindful of approaching age'?"

19 The Master said: "I was not born to understanding. I loved the past, and questioned it earnestly."

20 The Master never spake of ghosts or strength, crime or spirits.

21 The Master said: "Walking three together I am sure of teachers. I pick out the good and follow it; I see the bad and shun it."

[5] An abstruse, ancient classic, usually called the Book of Changes.

22 The Master said: "Heaven planted worth in me; what harm can come of Huan T´ui?"[6]

23 The Master said: "My boys, do ye think that I hide things from you? I hide nothing. One who keeps from his boys nought that he does, such is Ch´iu."[7]

24 The four things the Master taught were culture, conduct, faithfulness, and truth.

25 The Master said: "A holy man I shall not live to see; enough could I find a gentleman! A good man I shall not live to see; enough could I find a steadfast one! But when nothing poses as something, cloud as substance, want as riches, steadfastness must be rare."

26 The Master angled, but did not fish with a net; he shot, but not at birds sitting.

27 The Master said: "There may be men who act without understanding why. I do not. To listen much, pick out the good and follow it; to see much and ponder it: this comes next to understanding."

28 It was ill talking to the Hu villagers. A lad having been admitted, the disciples wondered.

[6]In B.C. 495, during Confucius' wanderings, Huan T´ui was an officer of Sung. He sent a band of men to kill Confucius; but why he did so is not clear.
[7]Confucius.

The Master said: "I allow his coming, not what is to come. Why be so harsh? If a man cleanse himself to gain admission, I admit his cleanness, but go not bail for his past."

29 The Master said: "Is love so far a thing? I yearn for love, and lo! love is come."

30 A judge of Ch´en asked whether Duke of Chao[8] knew courtesy.

Confucius answered: "He knew courtesy."

After Confucius had left, the judge beckoned Wu-ma Ch´i[9] to his side, and said: "I had heard that gentlemen are of no party, but are they too for party? The prince married a Wu, of the same name as himself, and called her Miss Tzu of Wu. If the prince knew courtesy, who does not know courtesy?"

When Wu-ma Ch´i told this to the Master, he said: "How lucky I am! If I make a slip, men are sure to know it!"

31 When any one sang to the Master, and sang well, he would make him repeat it and join in.

32 The Master said: "I have no more culture than others: to live as a gentleman is not yet mine."

---

[8]Duke Chao of Lu (+B.C. 510) was the duke who first employed Confucius. It is contrary to Chinese custom for a man to marry a girl of the same surname as himself.
[9]A disciple of Confucius.

33 The Master said: "How dare I lay claim to holiness or love? A man of endless craving I might be called, an unflagging teacher; but nothing more."

"That is just what we disciples cannot learn," said Kung-hsi Hua.

34 The Master being very ill, Tzu-lu asked leave to pray.

The Master said: "Is it the custom?"

"It is," answered Tzu-lu. "The Memorials say, 'Pray to the spirits in heaven above and on earth below.'"

The Master said: "Long lasting has my prayer been."

35 The Master said: "Waste begets self-will; thrift begets meanness: but better be mean than self-willed."

36 The Master said: "A gentleman is calm and spacious: the vulgar are always fretting."

37 The Master was friendly, yet dignified; he inspired awe, but not fear; he was respectful, yet easy.

1 THE MASTER SAID: "T´ai-po[1] might indeed be called a man of highest worth. Thrice he gave up the throne. Men were at a loss how to praise him."

2 The Master said: "Without a sense of courtesy, attentions grow into fussiness, heed turns to fearfulness, courage becomes unruliness, uprightness turns to harshness. When the gentry are true to kinsmen, love will thrive among the people. If they do not forsake old friends, the people will not be selfish."

---

[1]T´ai-po was the eldest son of the King of Chou. The father wished his third son to succeed him, in order that the throne might pass through him to his famous son, afterwards known as King Wen. To facilitate this plan T´ai-po and his second brother went into voluntary exile.

3   When Tseng-tzu lay sick he summoned his disciples and said: "Uncover my feet, uncover my arms. The poem says:

> 'As though a deep gulf
> Were yawning below,
> As crossing thin ice,
> Take heed how ye go.'

Till this day, and beyond, I have walked unscathed, my boys."[2]

4   When Tseng-tzu lay sick Meng Ching[3] came to ask after him.

Tseng-tzu said: "When a bird is to die, his note is sad; when a man is to die, his words are true. There are three duties that a gentleman prizes: to banish from his bearing violence and levity; to sort his face to the truth; to purge his speech of the low and unfair. As for temple matters, there are officers to mind them."

5   Tseng-tzu said: "Out of knowledge to learn from ignorance, out of wealth to learn from penury; having to seem wanting, real to seem shadow; when gainsaid never answering back: I had once a friend who would act thus."[4]

---

[2]The Chinese say: "The body is born whole by the mother; it is for the son to return it again whole."
[3]Head of the Meng clan, minister of Lu.
[4]This is believed to refer to Yen Yüan.

6 Tseng-tzu said: "A man to whom an orphan stripling or the fate of an hundred townships may be entrusted, and whom no crisis can corrupt, is he not a gentleman, a gentleman indeed?"

7 Tseng-tzu said: "The scholar had need be strong and bold; for his burden is heavy, the road is far. His burden is love, is it not a heavy one? Death is the goal, is that not far?"

8 The Master said: "Poetry rouses, courtesy upholds us, music is our crown."

9 The Master said: "The people may be made to follow: they cannot be made to understand."

10 The Master said: "Love of daring, inflamed by poverty, leads to crime: a man without love, if deeply ill-treated, will turn to crime."

11 The Master said: "All the glorious gifts of the Duke of Chou,[5] if coupled with pride and meanness, would not be worth one glance."

12 The Master said: "A man to whom three years of study have borne no fruit would be hard to find."

[5]See note to 7.5.

13 The Master said: "A man who loves learning with simple faith, who to mend his life is content to die, will not enter a tottering kingdom, nor stay in a land distraught. When right prevails below heaven, he is seen; when wrong prevails, he is unseen. When right prevails, he would blush to be poor and lowly; when wrong prevails, wealth and honours would shame him."

14 The Master said: "When not in office, discuss not policy."

15 The Master said: "In the first days of the music master Chih how grand was the ending of the Kuan-chü! How it filled the ear!"

16 The Master said: "Of such as are eager, but not straight; shallow, but not simple; dull, but not truthful, I will know nothing."

17 The Master said: "Study as though the time were short, as one who fears to lose."

18 The Master said: "It was sublime how Shun and Yü swayed the world and made light of it!"

19 The Master said: "How great was Yao in kingship! Sublime! Heaven alone is great; Yao alone was patterned on it! Boundless! Men's words failed them. Sublime the work he did, dazzling the wealth of his culture!"

20 Shun had five ministers, and order reigned below heaven.

King Wu said: "Ten in number are my able ministers."

Confucius said: "'The dearth of talent,' is not that the truth? The days when Yü[6] succeeded T´ang[7] were rich in talent; yet there were but nine men in all, and one of these was a woman. The utmost worth was the worth of Chou![8] Lord of two-thirds of the earth, he submitted all to Yin."

21 The Master said: "I find no flaw in Yü. Frugal in eating and drinking, he was lavish to the ghosts of the dead: ill-clad, he was gorgeous in cap and gown: his home a hovel, he poured out his strength upon dikes and ditches. No kind of flaw can I find in Yü."

[6]Shun.
[7]Yao.
[8]King Wen, Duke of Chou.

1   THE MASTER SELDOM spake of gain, doom, or love.

2   A man from the Ta-hsiang village said: "The great Confucius, with his vast learning, has made no name in anything."

When the Master heard it, he said to his disciples: "What shall I take up? Shall I take up charioteering? Shall I take up bowmanship? I must take up charioteering."

3   The Master said: "A linen cap is correct: to-day silk is worn. It is cheap, and I follow the many. To bow below is correct: to-day it is done above. This is over-weening, and, despite the many, I bow below."

4   From four things the Master was quite free. He had no by-views; he knew not "must," or "shall," or "I."

5 When the Master was affrighted in K´uang,[1] he said: "Since the death of King Wen, is not this the home of culture? Had Heaven condemned culture, later mortals had missed their share in it. If Heaven uphold culture, what can the men of K´uang do to me?"

6 A high minister said to Tzu-kung: "The Master must be a holy man, he can do so many things!"

Tzu-kung said: "Heaven has indeed well-nigh endowed him with holiness, and he is many-sided too."

When the Master heard it, he said: "Does the minister know me? Being lowly born, I learned many an humble trade in my youth. But has a gentleman skill in many things? No, in few things."

Lao said that the Master would say: "Having no post, I learned a craft."

7 The Master said: "Have I in truth understanding? I have no understanding. But if a yokel ask me aught in an empty way, I tap it on this side and that, and sift it to the bottom."

8 The Master said: "The phoenix comes not, nor does the river give forth a sign. All is over with me!"

---

[1]During the Master's wanderings. K´uang is said to have been a small state near Lu, that had been oppressed by Yang Huo. Confucius resembled him, and the men of K´uang set upon him, mistaking him for their enemy.

9 When the Master saw folk clad in mourning, or in robes of state, or else a blind man, he made a point of rising—even for the young—or, if he were passing by, of quickening his step.

10 Yen Yüan heaved a sigh and said: "As I gaze it grows higher, more remote as I dig! I sight it in front, next moment astern! The Master tempts men forward deftly bit by bit. He widened me with culture, he bound me with courtesy. Until my strength was spent I had no power to stop. The goal seemed at hand: I longed to reach it, but the way was closed."

11 When the Master was very ill, Tzu-lu moved the disciples to act as ministers.

During a better spell the Master said: "Yu has long been feigning. This show of ministers, when I have no ministers, whom can it deceive? Will it deceive Heaven? Moreover, is it not better to die in your arms, my boys, than to die in the arms of ministers? And if I lack a grand burial, shall I die by the roadside?"

12 Tzu-kung said: "Were a beauteous jadestone mine, ought I to hide it away in a case, or seek a good price and sell it?"

The Master said: "Sell it, sell it! I tarry for my price."

13 The Master wished to make his home among the nine tribes.[2]

One said: "They are low, how could ye?"

The Master said: "Where a gentleman has his home, can aught live that is low?"

14 The Master said: "After I came back from Wei to Lu the music was set straight and each song found its place."

15 The Master said: "To serve men of high rank when abroad, and father and brothers when at home; to dread slackness in graveside duties, and be no thrall to wine: to which of these have I won?"

16 As he stood by a stream, the Master said: "Hasting away like this, day and night without stop!"

17 The Master said: "I have found none who love good as they love women."

18 The Master said: "In making a mound, if I stop when one basketful more would end it, it is I that stop. In levelling ground, if I go on after throwing down one basketful, it is I that proceed."

---

[2]The half-barbarous tribes in the mountainous, eastern districts of the present province of Shantung.

19 The Master said: "Never listless when spoken to, such was Hui!"[3]

20 Speaking of Yen Yüan, the Master said: "The pity of it! I have seen him go on, but never have I seen him stop."

21 The Master said: "Some sprouts do not blossom, some blossoms bear no fruit."

22 The Master said: "Awe is due to youth. May not to-morrow be bright as to-day? To men of forty or fifty, who are unknown still, no awe is due."

23 The Master said: "Who would not give ear to a down-right word? But to mend is of price. Who would not be pleased by a guiding word? But to ponder the word is of price. With such as give ear, but will not mend; who are pleased, but will not ponder, I can do nothing."

24 The Master said: "Make faithfulness and truth thy masters: have no friends unlike thyself: be not ashamed to mend thy faults."

25 The Master said: "Three armies may be robbed of their leader, no wretch can be robbed of his will."

[3]Yen Yüan.

26 The Master said: "Clad in a tattered, quilted cloak, Yu[4] will stand unabashed amidst robes of fox and badger.

> 'Void of hatred and greed,
> What but good does he do?'"

But when Tzu-lu was ever humming these words, the Master said: "This is the way: but is it the whole of goodness?"

27 The Master said: "Erst the cold days show how fir and cypress are last to fade."

28 The Master said: "The wise are free from doubt; love is never vexed; the bold have no fears."

29 The Master said: "With some we can join in learning, but not in aims; with others we can join in aims, but not in standpoint; and with others again in standpoint, but not in measures."

> "The flowers overhead
> Are dancing in play;
> My thoughts are with thee,
> In thy home far away."

The Master said: "Her thoughts were not with him, or how could he be far away?"

4Tzu-lu.

1   AMONGST HIS OWN country folk Confucius wore a homely look, like one who has no word to say.

In the ancestral temple and at court his speech was full, but cautious.

2   At court, he talked frankly to men of low rank, winningly to men of high rank.

In the king's presence he looked intent and solemn.

3   When the king bade him receive guests, his face seemed to change, his knees to bend. He bowed left and right to those beside him, straightened his robes in front and behind, and sped forward, his elbows spread like wings. When the guest had left, he always reported it, saying: "The guest has ceased to look back."

4 Entering the palace gate he stooped, as though it were too low for him. He did not stand in the middle of the gate, nor step on the threshold.

Passing the throne, his face seemed to change, his knees to bend, he spake with bated breath.

Mounting the däis, he lifted his robes, bowed his back and masked his breathing, till it seemed to stop.

Coming down, his face relaxed below the first step, and bore a pleased look. From the foot of the steps he sped forward, his elbows spread like wings; and when again in his seat he looked intent as before.

5 When bearing the sceptre, his back bent, as under too heavy a burden. He held his hands not higher than in bowing, nor lower than in giving a present. He wore an awed look and dragged his feet, as though they were fettered.

When presenting royal gifts his manner was formal; but he was cheerful at the private audience.

6 This gentleman was never arrayed in maroon or scarlet; even at home he would not don red or purple.

In hot weather he wore unlined linen clothes, but always over other garments.

Over lamb-skin he wore black, over fawn he wore white, over foxskin he wore yellow. At home he wore a long fur robe, with the right sleeve short.

He always had his nightgown half as long again as his body.

In the house he wore fox or badger skin for warmth.

When out of mourning there was nothing wanting from his girdle.

Except for court dress, he was sparing of stuff.

He did not wear lamb's fur, or a black cap, on a visit of condolence.

On the first day of the moon he always went to court in court dress.

7 On fast days he always donned clothes of pale hue, changed his food, and moved from his wonted seat.

8 He did not dislike his rice cleaned with care, nor his hash chopped small.

He did not eat sour or mouldy rice, putrid fish, or tainted meat. Aught discoloured, or high, badly cooked, or out of season, he would not eat. He would not eat what was badly cut, or a dish with the wrong sauce. A choice of meats could not tempt him to eat more than he had a relish for. To wine alone he set no limit, but he did not drink till he got fuddled.

He did not drink bought wine, or eat ready-dried market meat.

Ginger was never missing at table.

He did not eat much.

After sacrifice at the palace he would not keep the meat over night, at home not more than three days. If kept longer it was not eaten.

He did not talk at meals, nor speak when in bed.

Though there were but coarse rice and vegetable soup, he made his offering with all reverence.

9 If his mat were not straight, he would not sit down.

10 When drinking with the villagers, as those with staves left, he left too.

At the village exorcisms he donned court dress, and stood on the eastern steps.

11 When sending inquiries to another land, he bowed twice and saw his messenger out.

On K´ang making him a gift of medicine, he accepted it with a bow, saying: "I do not know it: I dare not taste it."

12 His stables having been burnt, the Master, on his return from court, said: "Is any one hurt?" He did not ask after the horses.

13 When the king sent him bake-meat, he set his mat straight, and tasted it first. When the king sent him raw meat, he had it cooked for sacrifice. When the king sent a living beast, he had him reared.

When dining in attendance on the king, the king made the offering, Confucius ate of things first.

On the king coming to see him in sickness, he turned his face to the east and had his court dress spread across him, with the girdle over it.

When summoned by the king, he walked, without waiting for his carriage.

14 On entering the Great Temple he asked how each thing was done.

15 When a friend died who had no home to go to, he said: "It is for me to bury him."

When a friend sent a gift, even of a carriage and horses, he did not bow. He only bowed for sacrificial meat.

16 He did not sleep like a corpse. At home he unbent.

On meeting a mourner, and were he a friend, his face changed. Even in everyday clothes, when he met any one in full dress, or a blind man, his face grew staid.

When he met men in mourning he bowed over the cross-bar; to the census-bearers he bowed over the cross-bar.

Before choice meats he rose with changed look. At sharp thunder, or fierce wind, his look changed.

17 In mounting his chariot he stood straight and grasped the cord. When in his chariot he did not look round, speak fast, or point.

18 Seeing a man's face, she rose, flew round and settled.

The Master said: "Hen pheasant on the ridge, it is the season, it is the season."

He and Tzu-lu got on the scent thrice and then she rose.

1   THE MASTER SAID: "Those who led the way in courtesy and music are deemed rude, and elegant the later school of courtesy and music. My wont is to follow the leaders."

2   The Master said: "None of the men who were with me in Ch'en or Ts'ai come any more to my door! Of noble life were Yen Yüan, Min Tzu-ch'ien, Jan Po-niu, and Chung-kung; Tsai Wo and Tzu-kung were the talkers; statesmen Jan Yu and Chi-lu. Tzu-yu and Tzu-hsia were men of culture."

3   The Master said: "I get no help from Hui.[1] No word I say but delights him!"

---

[1]Yen Yüan.

4   The Master said: "How good a son was Min Tzu-ch´ien! In all that parents and brethren said of him no hole was picked."

5   Nan Jung would thrice repeat "The sceptre white."[2]

Confucius gave him his niece to wife.

6   Chi K´ang asked which of the disciples loved learning.

Confucius answered: "Yen Hui[3] loved learning. By ill luck his life was cut short. Now there is no one."

7   When Yen Yüan died, Yen Lu[4] asked for the Master's chariot to furnish an outer coffin.

The Master said: "Whether gifted or not, each one speaks of his son. When Li[5] died he had an inner but not an outer coffin. I would not walk on foot to furnish an outer coffin. Following in the wake of the ministry, it would ill become me to walk on foot."

8   When Yen Yüan died the Master cried: "Woe is me! I am undone of Heaven! I am undone of Heaven!"

---

[2]The verse runs—
> "A flaw can be ground
> From a sceptre white;
> A slip of the tongue
> No man can right."

[3]Yen Yüan.
[4]The father of Yen Yüan.
[5]Confucius' son.

9 When Yen Yüan died the Master gave way to grief.

Those with him said: "Sir, ye are giving way."

The Master said: "Am I giving way? If for this man I did not give way to grief, for whom should I give way?"

10 When Yen Yüan died the disciples wished to bury him in state.

The Master said: "This must not be."

The disciples buried him in state.

The Master said: "Hui treated me as a father: I have failed to treat him as a son. No, not I: it was your doing, my boys."

11 Chi-lu[6] asked what is due to the ghosts of the dead.

The Master said: "We fail in our duty to the living; can we do our duty to the dead?"

He ventured to ask about death.

"We know not life," said the Master, "how can we know death?"

---

[6]Tzu-lu.

12 Seeing the disciple Min standing at his side in winning strength, Tzu-lu with war-like front, Jan Yu and Tzu-kung fresh and rank, the Master's heart was glad.

"A man like Yu,"[7] he said, "dies before his day."

13 The men of Lu were building the Long Treasury.

Min Tzu-ch´ien said: "Would not the old one do? Why must a new one be built?"

The Master said: "That man does not talk: when he speaks, he hits the mark."

14 The Master said: "What has the lute of Yu[8] to do twanging at my door!"

But when the disciples began to look down on Tzu-lu, the Master said: "Yu has climbed to the hall, though he has not passed the closet door."

15 Tzu-kung asked whether Shih[9] or Shang[10] were the better man.

---

[7]Tzu-lu. This prophecy came true. Tzu-lu and Tzu-kao were officers of Wei when troubles arose. Tzu-lu hastened to the help of his master. He met Tzu-kao withdrawing from the danger, and was advised to follow suit. But Tzu-lu refused to desert the man whose pay he drew. He plunged into the fight and was killed.

[8]Tzu-lu.

[9]The disciple Tzu-chang.

[10]The disciple Tzu-hsia.

The Master said: "Shih goes too far: Shang goes not far enough."

"Then Shih is the better man," said Tzu-kung.

"Too far," replied the Master, "is no better than not far enough."

16 The Chi was richer than the Duke of Chou: Ch'iu[11] added to his wealth by becoming his taxgatherer.

The Master said: "He is no disciple of mine. Sound your drums to the attack, my boys!"

17 Ch'ai[12] is simple, Shen[13] is dull, Shih[14] is smooth, Yu[15] is coarse.

18 The Master said: "Hui[16] is well-nigh faultless, and oft-times empty. Tz'u[17] will not bow to fate, and hoards up substance; but his views are often sound."

19 Tzu-chang asked, What is the way of a good man?

The Master said: "He does not tread in footprints; neither can he gain the closet."

---

[11] The disciple Jan Yu.
[12] The disciple Kao Ch'ai.
[13] The disciple Tseng-tzu.
[14] The disciple Tzu-chang.
[15] Tzu-lu.
[16] The disciple Yen Yüan.
[17] The disciple Tzu-kung.

20 The Master said: "Commend a man for plain speaking: he may prove a gentleman, or else but seeming honest."

21 Tzu-lu asked: "Shall I do all I am taught?"

The Master said: "Whilst thy father and elder brothers live, how canst thou do all thou art taught?"

Jan Yu asked: "Shall I do all I am taught?"

The Master said: "Do all thou art taught."

Kung-hsi Hua said: "Yu[18] asked, 'Shall I do all I am taught?' and ye spake, Sir, of father and elder brothers. Ch´iu[19] asked, 'Shall I do all I am taught?' and ye answered, 'Do all thou art taught.' I am puzzled, and make bold to ask you, Sir."

The Master said: "Ch´iu is bashful, so I egged him on: Yu has the pluck of two, so I held him back."

22 When fear beset the Master in K´uang, Yen Yüan fell behind.

The Master said: "I held thee as dead."

He answered: "Whilst my Master lives durst I brave death?"

---

[18]Tzu-lu.
[19]Jan Yu.

23 Chi Tzu-jan[20] asked whether Chung Yu[21] or Jan Ch'iu[22] could be called statesmen.

The Master said: "I thought ye would ask me some riddle, Sir, and your text is Yu[21] and Ch'iu.[22] A minister who does his duty to the king, and withdraws rather than do wrong, is called a statesman. As for Yu and Ch'iu, I should call them tools."

"Who would do one's bidding them?"

"Neither would they do your bidding," said the Master, "if bidden slay king or father."

24 Tzu-lu had Tzu-kao made governor of Pi.

The Master said: "Thou art undoing a man's son."

Tzu-lu said: "What with the people and the guardian spirits must a man read books to come by knowledge?"

The Master said: "This is why I hate a glib tongue."

25 The Minister said to Tzu-lu, Tseng Hsi,[23] Jan Yu, and Kung-hsi Hua as they sat beside him: "I may be a day older than you, but forget that. Ye are wont to say, 'I am unknown.' Well, had ye a name, what would; ye do?"

---

[20] The younger brother of Chi Huan, head of the Chi clan.
[21] Tzu-lu. He and Jan Yu had taken office under the Chi.
[22] Jan Yu.
[23] A disciple: the father of Tseng-tzu.

Tzu-lu lightly answered: "Give me charge of a land of a thousand chariots, crushed between great neighbours, overrun by soldiery and searched by famine, in three years' time I could put courage into the people and high purpose."

The Master smiled.

"What wouldst thou do, Ch'iu?"[24] he said.

He answered: "Had I charge of sixty or seventy square miles, or from fifty to sixty square miles, in three years' time I would give the people plenty. As for courtesy, music, and the like, they would wait the rise of a gentleman."

"And what wouldst thou do, Ch'ih?"[25]

He answered: "I speak of the things I fain would learn, not of what I can do. At service in the Ancestral Temple, or at the Grand Audience, clad in black robe and cap, I fain would fill a small part."

"And what wouldst thou do, Tien?"[26]

Tien ceased to play, pushed his still sounding lute aside, rose and answered: "My choice would be unlike those of the other three."

"What harm in that?" said the Master. "Each but spake his mind."

[24]Jan Yu.
[25]Kung-hsi Hua.
[26]Tseng Hsi.

"In the last days of spring, all clad for the season, with five or six grown men and six or seven lads, I would bathe in the Yi, be fanned by the breeze in the Rain God's glade, and wander home with song."

The Master sighed and said: "I hold with Tien."

Tseng Hsi stayed after the other three had left, and said: "What did ye think of what the others said, Sir?"

"Each but spake his mind," said the Master.

"Why did ye smile at Yu,[27] Sir?"

"Lands are swayed by courtesy, but what he said was not modest. That was why I smiled."

"But did not Ch'iu, too, speak of a state?"

"Where could sixty or seventy square miles be found, or from fifty to sixty, that are not a state?"

"And did not Ch'ih, too, speak of a state?"

"Who but great vassals would there be in the Ancestral Temple, or at the Grand Audience? But if Ch'ih were to play a small part, who could fill a big one?"

[27]Tzu-lu.

12

1 YEN YÜAN ASKED, What is love?

The Master said: "Love is to conquer self and turn to courtesy. Could we conquer self and turn to courtesy for but one day, all mankind would turn to love. Does love flow from within, or does it flow from others?"

Yen Yüan said: "May I ask what are its signs?"

The Master said: "To be ever courteous of eye and ever courteous of ear; to be ever courteous in word and ever courteous in deed."

Yen Yüan said: "Dull as I am, I hope to live by these words."

2   Chung-kung asked, What is love?

The Master said: "Without the door to behave as though a great guest were come; to treat the people as though we tendered the high sacrifice; not to do unto others what we would not they should do unto us; to breed no wrongs in the state and breed no wrongs in the home."

Chung-kung said: "Dull as I am, I hope to live by these words."

3   Ssu-ma Niu[1] asked, What is love?

The Master said: "Love is slow to speak."

"To be slow to speak! Can that be called love?"

The Master said: "That which is hard to do, can it be lightly spoken?"

4   Ssu-ma Niu asked, What is a gentleman?

The Master said: "A gentleman knows neither sorrow nor fear."

"No sorrow and no fear! Can that be called a gentleman?"

The Master said: "He finds no sin in his heart, so why should he sorrow, what should he fear?"

5   Ssu-ma Niu cried sadly: "All men have brothers, I alone have none!"

[1]A disciple.

Tzu-hsia said: "I have heard that life and death are allotted, that wealth and honours are in Heaven's hand. A gentleman is careful and does not trip; he is humble towards others and courteous. All within the four seas are brethren; how can a gentleman mourn his lack of them?"

6 Tzu-chang asked, What is insight?

The Master said: "To be unmoved by lap and wash of slander, or by plaints that pierce to the quick, may be called insight. Yea, whom lap and wash of slander, or plaints that pierce to the quick cannot move may be called far-sighted."

7 Tzu-kung asked, What is kingcraft?

The Master said: "Food enough, troops enough, and a trusting people."

Tzu-kung said: "Were there no help for it, which could best be spared of the three?"

"Troops," said the Master.

"And were there no help for it, which could better be spared of the other two?"

"Food," said the Master. "From of old all men die, but without trust a people cannot stand."

8 Chi Tzu-ch´eng[2] said: "A gentleman is all nature: what can art do for him?"

[2]Minister of Wei.

"Alas! my lord," said Tzu-kung, "how ye speak of a gentleman! No team overtakes the tongue! Nature is no more than art; art is no more than nature. Without the fur, a tiger or a leopard's hide is as the hide of a dog, or goat."

9 Duke Ai said to Yu Jo[3]: "In this year of dearth I have not enough for my wants; what should be done?"

"Ye might tithe the people," answered Yu Jo.

"A fifth is all too little," said the duke; "how could a tenth avail?"

"When the people all live in plenty," answered Yu Jo, "will the king alone be in want? If the people are all in want, can the king alone live in plenty?"

10 Tzu-chang asked how to raise the mind and scatter delusions.

The Master said: "Make faithfulness and truth thy masters, and follow the right; the mind will be raised. We wish life to things we love, death to things we hate. To wish them both life and death is a delusion.

> 'Whether prompted by wealth,
> Yet ye made a distinction.'"

11 Ching,[4] Duke of Ch´i asked Confucius, What is kingcraft?

---

[3] A disciple of Confucius.
[4] Confucius was in Ch´i in B.C. 517. The duke was overshadowed by his ministers, and contemplated setting aside his eldest son.

Confucius answered: "When the king is king and the minister is minister; when the father is father and the son is son."

"True indeed!" said the duke. "Were the king no king and the minister no minister, were the father no father and the son no son, could I get aught to eat, though the grain were there?"

12 The Master said: "To stint a quarrel with half a word Yu[5] is the man."

Tzu-lu never slept over a promise.

13 The Master said: "At hearing lawsuits I am no better than another. What is needed is to stay lawsuits."

14 Tzu-chang asked, What is kingcraft?

The Master said: "To be tireless of spirit and faithful at work."

15 The Master said: "Breadth of reading and the ties of courtesy will also keep a man from error's path."

16 The Master said: "A gentleman shapes the good in man; he does not shape the bad in him. Contrariwise the vulgar."

17 Chi K´ang[6] asked Confucius how to rule.

---

[5]Tzu-lu.
[6]On the death of Chi Huan, Chi K´ang set aside his infant nephew and made himself head of the clan.

Confucius answered: "To rule is to set straight. If we give an upright lead, sir, who will dare walk crooked?"

18 Chi K´ang being vexed by robbers spake of it to Confucius.

Confucius answered: "But for your greed, sir, though ye rewarded thieves, no man would steal."

19 Chi K´ang, speaking of kingcraft, said to Confucius: "To help the good, should we kill the bad?"

Confucius answered: "Sir, what need has a ruler to kill? Were ye set on good, sir, your people would do good. The king's mind is the wind, and grass are the minds of the people: whither the wind blows, thither the grass bends."

20 Tzu-chang asked, When may a scholar be called eminent?

The Master said: "What dost thou mean by eminence?"

Tzu-chang answered: "To be famous in the state, and famous in his home."

The Master said: "That is fame, not eminence. The eminent man is plain and straight. He loves right, weighs men's words, and scans their looks. At pains to step down to them, he will be eminent in the state, and eminent in his home. The famous man wears a mask of love, but his deeds belie it. He knows no misgivings, and fame will be his in the state and fame be his in his home."

21 Whilst wandering through the Rain God's glade with the Master, Fan Ch'ih said to him: "May I ask how to raise the mind, amend evil, and scatter errors?"

The Master said: "A good question! Rate the task above the prize; will not the mind be raised? Fight thine own faults, not the faults of others; will not evil be mended? One angry morning to forget both self and kin, is that no error?"

22 Fan Ch'ih asked, What is love?

The Master said: "To love mankind."

He asked, What is wisdom?

The Master said: "To know mankind."

Fan Ch'ih did not understand.

The Master said: "Exalt the straight, put aside the crooked; the crooked will grow straight."

Fan Ch'ih withdrew, and meeting Tzu-hsia, said to him: "I was received by the Master and asked him 'What is wisdom?' The Master answered: 'Exalt the straight, put aside the crooked; the crooked will grow straight.' What did he mean?"

"How rich a saying!" said Tzu-hsia. "When Shun[7] was lord of the earth, he chose Kao-yao from the many,

7An emperor of the golden age.

exalted him, and evil vanished. When T'ang[8] was lord of the earth, he chose Yi-yin[9] from the many, exalted him, and evil vanished."

23 Tzu-kung asked about friends.

The Master said: "Talk faithfully to them: guide them with skill. If this prove vain, stop. Do not court shame."

24 Tseng-tzu said: "A gentleman gathers friends by culture and props love with friendship."

---

[8]The founder of the Shang, or Yin, dynasty.

[9]T'ang's chief minister. "Yi-yin said: 'Is he whom I serve not my king? Are they whom I lead not my people?' In quiet times he took office and in lawless times he took office. He said: 'Heaven begat mankind, meaning those who are quick learners to teach those slow to learn, and those who are quick-sighted to teach those slow to see. I am one of Heaven's men whose sight is quick: it falls to me to show the way to the people.' Were there man or wife below heaven, who had missed his share in the heritage of Yao and Shun, it was to him as though his hand had pushed him into the ditch; for the burden he took upon him was the weight of all below heaven." (Mencius, V. B. 1.)

1   TZU-LU ASKED how to rule.

The Master said: "Lead the way: take pains."

Asked to add more, he said: "Never flag."

2   When steward of the Chi, Chung-kung asked how to
rule.

The Master said: "Let officers act first: overlook small
faults: raise worth and talent."

Chung-kung said: "How shall I learn to know the worth
and talent I have to raise?"

"Raise those thou dost know," said the Master; "and
those unknown to thee, will other men pass by?"

3 Tzu-lu said: "The King of Wei[1] looks to you, Sir, to govern. How shall ye begin?"

"If need were," said the Master, "by putting names right."

"Indeed," said Tzu-lu, "that is far fetched, Sir! Why put them right?"

"Yu," said the Master, "thou art ill-bred. On matters beyond his ken a gentleman speaks with caution. If names are not right, words are misused. When words are misused, affairs go wrong. When affairs go wrong, courtesy and music droop. When courtesy and music droop, law and justice fail. And when law and justice fail them, a people can move neither hand nor foot. So a gentleman must be ready to put names into speech, to put words into deed. A gentleman is nowise careless of words."

4 Fan Ch'ih asked to be taught husbandry.

The Master said: "I cannot rank with an old husbandman."

He asked to be taught gardening.

The Master said: "I cannot rank with an old gardener."

After Fan Ch'ih had left, the Master said: "How small a man! If those above love courtesy, none will dare to slight them: if those above love right, none will dare to disobey: if those above love truth, none will dare to hide

[1]See note to 7.14. Tzu-lu was his officer.

the heart. Then, from the four corners of the earth, folk will gather, their children on their backs; what need will there be for husbandry?"

5 The Master said: "Though a man have conned three hundred poems; if he stand helpless when put to govern; if he cannot answer for himself, when sent to the four corners of the earth; despite their number, what have they done for him?"

6 The Master said: "The man of upright life is obeyed before he speaks; commands even go unheeded where the life is crooked."

7 The Master said: "The governments of Lu and Wei are brothers."

8 Speaking of Ching, of the ducal house of Wei, the Master said: "He was wise in his private life. When he had begun saving, he said, 'This is much.' When he grew better off, he said 'Now we lack nothing.' And when he was rich, he said 'We live in splendour.'"

9 Whilst Jan Yu was driving him on the road to Wei, the Master said: "What numbers!"

Jan Yu said: "Since numbers are here, what next is needed?"

"Wealth," said the Master.

"And after wealth, what next were needed?"

"Teaching," said the Master.

10 The Master said: "Had I power for a twelvemonth only, much could be done. In three years all were ended."

11 The Master said: "'Could good men govern for an hundred years, cruelty would be vanquished, putting to death an end.' How true are these words!"

12 The Master said: "Had we a king among men, a lifetime would pass ere love dawned!"

13 The Master said: "What is governing to him who can rule himself? Who cannot rule himself, how should he rule others?"

14 As the disciple Jan[2] came back from court, the Master said to him: "Why so late?"

"Business of state kept me," he answered.

"Household business," said the Master. "Though I am out of office, I had heard were there business of state."

15 Duke Ting asked: "Is there any one saying that can prosper a kingdom?"

Confucius answered: "That is more than words can do. But a proverb says `Hard it is to be king, nor yet light to be minister.' And did one know how hard it is to be king, might not this saying all but prosper a kingdom?"

---

[2]Jan Yu. He was in the service of the Chi, not of the Duke of Lu.

"And is there any one saying that can wreck a kingdom?"

"That is more than words can do," Confucius answered. "But a proverb says 'My one joy as king is that none withstand what I say.' Now if none withstand him when right, will it not be well? But if none withstand him when wrong, might not this saying all but wreck a kingdom?"

16 The Duke of She asked, What is kingcraft?

The Master said: "To gladden those around us and draw men from afar."

17 Tzu-hsia, when governor of Chü-fu, asked how to rule.

The Master said: "Never be in a hurry. shut thine eyes to small gains. Nought done in a hurry is thorough, and an eye for small gain means big things undone."

18 The Duke of She told Confucius: "Among the upright men of my home if the father steal a sheep his son will bear witness."

Confucius answered: "Our people's uprightness is unlike that. The father screens his son, the son screens his father. There is uprightness in this."

19 Fan Ch'ih asked, What is love?

The Master said: "To be respectful at home, painstaking at work, faithful to all. Even among savages none of this may be dropped."

20 Tzu-kung asked, When can a man be called a good crown servant?

The Master said: "In private life he wants a sense of shame; if sent to the four corners of the earth he must not disgrace the king's commands."

"May I ask who would rank second?"

"A man who his clansmen call dutiful, and his neighbours call modest."

"May I ask who would rank next?"

"A man who clings to his word and sticks to his course, a flinty little fellow, would perhaps come next."

"And how are the crown servants of to-day?"

"What! The weights and measures men!" said the Master. "Are they worth reckoning?"

21 The Master said: "As followers of the golden mean are not to be found, I have to work with ambitious and headstrong men. Ambitious men push ahead, and there are things that headstrong men will not do."

22 The Master said: "The men of the south say, 'Unless steadfast a man will make neither a wizard nor a leech.' This is true. 'A falling off in merit will reap disgrace.'"

The Master said: "Neglect of the omens, that is all."

23 The Master said: "A gentleman is pleasant, not fulsome: the vulgar are fulsome, but not pleasant."

24 Tzu-kung said: "Would it be right if a man were liked by all his neighbours?"

"No," said the Master.

"And would it be right if a man were hated by all his neighbours?"

"No," said the Master. "It would be better if the good men of the neighbourhood liked him, and the bad men of the neighbourhood hated him."

25 The Master said: "A gentleman is easy to serve, and hard to please. Nought but what is right pleases him: he fits his behests to the man. The vulgar are hard to serve, and easy to please. What is wrong may yet please them: but of their men they expect all things."

26 The Master said: "A gentleman is high-minded, not proud: the vulgar are proud, but not high-minded."

27 The Master said: "Strength and courage, simplicity and meekness are akin to love."

28 Tzu-lu asked, When can a man be called educated?

The Master said: "A man who is earnest, encouraging, and kind may be called educated. Earnest with friends and encouraging; kind towards his brothers."

29 The Master said: "Could a good man teach the people for seven years, they would be fit for arms also."

30 The Master said: "To take untaught men into battle is to cast them away."

1 HSIEN[1] ASKED, What is shame?

The Master said: "Hire when right prevails, hire when wrong prevails, hire is always shame."

2 "To eschew strife and boasting, spite and greed, can that be called love?"

The Master said: "I call that hard to do: I do not know that it is love."

3 The Master said: "A scholar who loves comfort is not worthy the name."

[1]The disciple Yüan Ssu.

4 The Master said: "When right prevails, be fearless of speech and fearless in deed: when wrong prevails, be fearless in deed but soft of speech."

5 The Master said: "A man of worth can always talk, but talkers are not always men of worth. Love is always bold, though boldness is found without love."

6 Nan-kung Kuo said to Confucius: "Yi[2] was good at archery, Ao could push a boat overland; each died before his time. Yü and Chi toiled at their crops, and won the world."

The Master did not answer.

But when Nan-kung Kuo had left, the Master said: "What a gentleman he is! How he prizes worth!"

7 The Master said: "Gentlemen without love there may be, but the vulgar must ever be strangers to love."

8 The Master said: "Can one love, yet take no pains? Can he be faithful who gives no counsel?"

9 The Master said: "The decrees were drafted by P´i Shen, criticised by Shih-shu, polished by the Foreign Minister Tzu-yü, and given the final touches by Tzu-ch´an of Tung-li."

---

[2]Yi was killed by his best pupil, who thought within himself. "In all the world Yi alone shoots better than I," and so he slew him.

10   Being asked what he thought of Tzu-ch'an, the Master said: "A kind-hearted man."

Asked what he thought of Tzu-hsi, the Master said: "Of him! What I think of him!"

Asked what he thought of Kuan Chung,[3] the Master said: "He was the man who drove the Po from the town of Pien and its three hundred households, to end his days on coarse rice, and no word of wrong could he find to say."

11   The Master said: "It is hard not to chafe at poverty, a light thing not to be proud of wealth."

12   The Master said: "Meng Kung-ch'o is more than fit to be steward to Chao or Wei, but is not fit to be minister of T'eng or Hsieh."

13   Tzu-lu asked what were a full-grown man.

The Master said: "A man wise as Tsang Wu-chung, greedless as Kung-ch'o, bold as Chuang of Pien, skilful as Jan Ch'iu, and graced with courtesy and music, might be called a full-grown man. But to-day who asks the like of a full-grown man? Who in sight of gain remembers right, in face of danger will risk his life, and cleaves to his word for a lifetime, however old the bond, him we must call a full-grown man."

[3]See note to 3.22.

14 Speaking of Kung-shu Wen, the Master said to Kung-ming Chia: "Is it true that thy master does not speak, nor laugh, nor take a gift?"

Kung-ming Chia answered: "That is saying too much. My master speaks when it is time to speak, so none weary of his speaking: he laughs when he is merry, so none weary of his laughter: he takes what it is right to take, so none weary of his taking."

"It may be so," said the Master; "but is it?"

15 The Master said: "When Tsang Wu-chung holding Fang asked Lu to appoint an heir, though he said that he was not forcing his prince, I cannot believe it."

16 The Master said: "Duke Wen of Chin was deep, but dishonest: Duke Huan of Ch´i was honest, but shallow."

17 Tzu-lu said: "When Duke Huan slew the young duke Chiu, Shao Hu died with him, but not Kuan Chung, was this not want of love?"[4]

---

[4]Huan and Chiu were brothers, sons of the Duke of Ch´i. When the father died, their uncle seized the throne. To preserve the rightful heirs Shao Hu and Kuan Chung fled with Chiu to Lu, whilst Huan escaped to another state. The usurper having subsequently been murdered, Huan returned to Ch´i and secured the throne. He then required the Duke of Lu to kill his brother and deliver up to him Shao Hu and Kuan Chung. This was done. But on the way to Ch´i, Shao Hu cut his throat. Kuan Chung, on the other hand, took service under Duke Huan, became his Prime Minister, and raised the state to greatness (see note to 3.22).

The Master said: "Duke Huan gathered the nobles together, without help from chariots of war, through the might of Kuan Chung. What can love do more? What can love do more?"

18 Tzu-kung said: "In becoming minister, instead of dying with the young duke Chiu, when he was slain by Duke Huan, Kuan Chung showed want of love, it would seem."

The Master said: "Through Kuan Chung helping Duke Huan to bend the nobility, and tame the world, men have fared the better from that day unto this. But for Kuan Chung we should wear our hair down our backs and the left arm bare: or should he, like the ploughboy and his lass, their troth to keep, have drowned in a ditch, no man the wiser?"

19 The minister Hsien, once steward to Kung-shu Wen, went to audience of the duke together with Wen.

When the Master heard of this, he said: "He is rightly called Wen (cultured)."

20 The Master spake of the wickedness of Ling, Duke of Wei.

K´ang[5] said: "If that be so, how does he escape ruin?"

Confucius answered: "With Chung-shu Yü in charge of the guests, the reader T´o in charge of the Ancestral Temple, and Wang-sun Chia in charge of the troops, how should he come to ruin?"

[5]Chi K´ang.

2 1 The Master said: "If the tongue have no fear, words are hard to make good."

2 2 Ch´en Ch´eng murdered Duke Chien.[6]

Confucius cleansed himself, went to court, and told Duke Ai, saying: "Ch´en Heng has murdered his prince. Pray chastise him."

The duke said: "Tell the three chiefs."

Confucius said: "Following in the wake of the ministry I dared not leave this untold; but the prince says, 'Tell the three chiefs.'"

He told the three chiefs. It was vain.

Confucius said: "Following in the wake of the ministry I dared not leave this untold."

2 3 Tzu-lu asked how to serve the king.

The Master said: "Never cheat him: withstand him to the face."

2 4 The Master said: "A gentleman's life leads upwards; a vulgar life leads down."

2 5 The Master said: "Men of old learned for their own sake: the men of to-day learn for show."

---

[6]B.C. 481, two years before the death of Confucius, who was not at the time in office. Chien was Duke of Ch´i, a state bordering on Lu. The three chiefs were the heads of the three great clans, all powerful in Lu.

26 Ch´ü Po-yü sent an envoy to Confucius.

As they sat together, Confucius asked him: "How is your lord busied?"

He answered: "My lord tries to pare his faults, and tries in vain."

When the envoy had left, the Master said: "An envoy, an envoy indeed!"

27 The Master said: "When not in office discuss not policy."

28 Tseng-tzu said: "A gentleman is bent on keeping his place."

29 The Master said: "A gentleman is shamefast of speech: his deeds go further."

30 The Master said: "In three ways I fall short of a gentleman. Love is never vexed; wisdom has no doubts; courage is without fear."

Tzu-kung replied: "That is what ye say, Sir."

31 Tzu-kung would compare one man with another.

The Master said: "What talents Tz´u has! Now I have no time for this."

32 The Master said: "Sorrow not at being unknown: sorrow for thine own shortcomings."

33 The Master said: "Not to expect falsehood, nor look for mistrust, and yet to forestall them, shows worth in a man."

34 Wei-sheng Mou said: "How dost thou still find roosts to roost on, Ch´ıu, unless by wagging a glib tongue?"

Confucius answered: "I dare not wag a glib tongue; but I hate stubbornness."

35 The Master said: "A steed is not praised for his strength, but praised for his mettle."

36 One said: "To mete out good for evil, how were that?"

"And how would ye meet good?" said the Master. "Meet evil with justice: meet good with good."

37 The Master said: "Alas! no man knows me!"

Tzu-kung said: "Why do ye say, Sir, that no man knows you?"

The Master said: "Never murmuring against Heaven, nor finding fault with men; learning from the lowest, cleaving the heights. I am known but to one, but to Heaven."

38 Liao, the duke's uncle, spake ill of Tzu-lu to Chi-sun.[7]

Tzu-fu Ching-po told this to Confucius, saying: "My lord's mind is surely being led astray by the duke's uncle, but strength is yet mine to expose his body in the marketplace."

[7]The head of the Chi clan, in whose service Tzu-lu was.

The Master said: "The doom has fallen if truth is to win: it has fallen if truth is to lose. Can Liao, the duke's uncle, fight against doom?"

39 The Master said: "Men of worth shun the world; the next best shun the land. Then come men who go at a look, then men who go at speech."

40 The Master said: "Seven men did so."

41 Tzu-lu spent a night at Shih-men.

The gate-keeper asked him: "Whence comest thou?"

"From Confucius," he answered.

"The man who knows it is vain, yet cannot forbear to stir?" said the gate-keeper.

42 When the Master was chiming his sounding stones in Wei, a basket-bearer said, as he passed the door: "His heart is full, who chimes those stones!" But then he added: "For shame! What a tinkling note! If no one heed thee, have done!

> 'Wade the deep places,
> Lift thy robe through the shallows.'"

The Master said: "Where there's a will, that is lightly done."

43 Tzu-chang said: "What does the book mean by saying that Kao-tsung,[8] when mourning his predecessor, did not speak for three years?"

[8] An emperor of the house of Yin.

The Master said: "Why pick out Kao-tsung? Men of old were all thus. For three years after the king had died, the hundred officers acted each for himself, and obeyed the chief minister."

44 The Master said: "When those above love courtesy, the people are easy to lead."

45 Tzu-lu asked, What is a gentleman?

The Master said: "A man bent on shaping his mind."

"Is that all?" said Tzu-lu.

"Oh shaping his mind to give happiness to others."

"And is that all?"

"On shaping his mind to give happiness to the people," said the Master. "To shape the mind and give happiness to the people, for this both Yao and Shun still pined."

46 Yüan Jang awaited the Master squatting.

The Master said: "Unruly when young, unmentioned as man, undying when old, spells good-for-nothing!" and hit him on the leg with his staff.

47 When a lad from the village of Ch´üeh was made message-bearer, some one asked, saying: "Is it because he has made progress?"

The Master said: "I have seen him sitting in a man's seat, seen him walking abreast of his elders. This shows no wish to improve, only hurry to be a man."

1 LING, DUKE OF Wei, asked Confucius about the line of battle.

Confucius answered: "Of temple ware I have learned: arms I have not studied."

On the morrow he went his way.

In Ch'en grain ran out. His followers grew too ill to rise. Tzu-lu could not hide his vexation.

"Must gentlemen also face misery?" he said.

"Of course a gentleman must face misery," said the Master. "It goads the vulgar to violence."

2 The Master said: "Dost thou not think Tz'u,[1] that I am a man who learns much, and bears it in mind?"

[1]Tzu-kung.

"Yes," he answered: "is it not so?"

"No," said the Master. "I string all into one."

3   The Master said: "Yu,[2] how few know what is worthy!"

4   The Master said: "To rule doing nothing, that was Shun's way. What need to be doing? Self-respect and a kingly look are all."

5   Tzu-chang asked how to get on.

The Master said: "Be faithful and true of word; let thy walk be plain and lowly: thou wilt get on, though in savage land. If thy words be not faithful and true, thy walk plain and lowly, wilt thou get on, though in thine own home? Standing, see these words ranged before thee; driving, see them written upon the yoke. Then thou wilt get on."

Tzu-chang wrote them upon his girdle.

6   The Master said: "Straight indeed was the historian Yü! Straight as an arrow when right prevailed, and straight as an arrow when wrong prevailed! What a gentleman was Ch'ü Po-yü! When right prevailed he took office: when wrong prevailed he rolled himself up in thought."

---

[2]Tzu-lu: believed to have been said to him on the occasion mentioned above in 15.1.

7 The Master said: "To keep silence to him who has ears to hear is to spill the man. To speak to a man without ears to hear is to spill thy words. Wisdom spills neither man nor word."

8 The Master said: "A high will, or a loving heart, will not seek life at cost of love. To fulfil love they will kill the body."

9 Tzu-kung asked how to practise love.

The Master said: "A workman bent on good work will first sharpen his tools. In the land that is thy home, serve the best men in power, and get thee friends who love."

10 Yen Yüan asked how to rule a kingdom.

The Master said: "Follow the Hsia seasons; drive in the chariot of Yin; wear the head-dress of Chou; choose for music the Shao and its dance. Banish the strains of Cheng, and shun men of glib tongue; for wanton are the strains of Cheng; there is danger in a glib tongue."

11 The Master said: "Without thought for far off things, there will be troubles near at hand."

12 The Master said: "It is finished! I have met no one who loves good as he loves women!"

13 The Master said: "Did not Tsang Wen filch his post? He knew the worth of Liu-hsia Hui,[3] and did not stand by him."

14 The Master said: "By asking much of self, and throwing little on others, ill feeling is put to flight."

15 The Master said: "Unless a man ask, 'Will this help? will that help?' I know not how to help him."

16 The Master said: "When all day long there is no talk of right, and sharp moves find favour, the company is in hard case."

17 The Master said: "A gentleman makes right his base. Done with courtesy, spoken with deference, rounded with truth, right makes a gentleman."

18 The Master said: "His unworthiness vexes a gentleman: to live unknown cannot vex him."

19 The Master said: "A gentleman fears lest his name should die when life is done."

---

[3]Another of these *seigneurs du temps jadis* who is more to us than a dim shadow, still living on in the pages of Mencius. There we learn that "He was not ashamed of a foul king, nor scorned a small post. He hid not his worth in office, but held his own way. Dismissal did not vex him; want did not make him sad. If thrown together with countrymen he felt so much at ease that he could not bear to leave them. 'Thou art thou.' he said, 'and I am I. Standing beside me with shoulders bare, or body naked, how canst thou defile me?'"

20 The Master said: "A gentleman looks within: the vulgar look unto others."

21 The Master said: "A gentleman is firm, not quarrelsome; a friend, not a partisan."

22 The Master said: "A gentleman does not raise a man for his words, nor scorn what is said for the speaker."

23 Tzu-kung asked: "Can one word cover the whole duty of man?"

The Master said: "Fellow-feeling, perhaps. Do not do unto others what thou wouldst not they should do unto thee."

24 The Master said: "Of the men that I meet, whom do I decry? whom do I flatter? Or if I flatter, it is after trial. Because of this people three lines of kings followed the straight road."

25 The Master said: "Even in my time an historian would leave a blank in his text, an owner of a horse would lend him to others to ride. To-day it is so no more."

26 The Master said: "Honeyed words confound goodness: impatience of trifles confounds great projects."

27 The Master said: "The hatred of the many calls for search: the favour of the many calls for search."

28 The Master said: "The man can exalt the truth: truth cannot exalt the man."

29 The Master said: "The fault is to cleave to a fault."

30 The Master said: "In vain have I spent in thought whole days without food, whole nights without sleep! Study is better."

31 The Master said: "A gentleman aims at truth; he does not aim at food. Ploughing may end in famine; study may end in pay. But a gentleman pines for truth: he is not pined with poverty."

32 The Master said: "What the mind has won will be lost again, unless love hold it fast. A mind to understand and love to hold fast, without dignity of bearing, will go unhonoured. A mind to understand, love to hold fast and dignity of bearing are incomplete, without courteous ways."

33 The Master said: "A gentleman has no skill in trifles, but has strength for big tasks: the vulgar are skilled in trifles, but have no strength for big tasks."

34 The Master said: "Love is more to the people than fire and water. I have known men come to their death by fire and water: I have met no man whom love brought unto death."

35 The Master said: "When love is at stake yield not to an army."

36 The Master said: "A gentleman is consistent, not changeless."

37 The Master said: "A servant of the king honours work and rates pay last."

38 The Master said: "All educated men are peers."

39 The Master said: "Mingle not in projects with men whose ways are not thine."

40 The Master said: "The whole end of speech is to be understood."

41 When the music-master Mien was presented, the Master, on coming to the steps, said: "Here are the steps." On reaching the mat, the Master said: "Here is the mat." When all were seated, the Master told him: "Such an one is here, and such an one is here."

After the music-master had left, Tzu-chang said: "Is this the way to speak to a music-master?"

The Master said: "Surely it is the way to help a music-master."[4]

---

[4]The man being blind, like most musicians in the East.

16

1   THE CHI WAS about to chastise Chuan-yü.[1]

Jan Yu and Chi-lu,[2] being received by Confucius, said to him: "The Chi is going to deal with Chuan-yü."

Confucius said: "After all, Ch'iu,[3] are ye not in the wrong? The kings of old made Chuan-yü lord of Tung Meng.[4] It is within the borders of the realm, moreover, and a vassal state. Ought it to be chastised?"

Jan Yu said: "Our lord wishes it. We, his ministers, are both against it."

---

[1] A small feudatory state of Lu.
[2] Tzu-lu. He and Jan Yu were at the time in the service of the Chi.
[3] Jan Yu.
[4] A mountain in Chuan-yü. The ruler of that state, having received from the emperor the right to sacrifice to its mountains, had some measure of independence, though the state was feudatory to Lu, and within its borders.

Confucius said: "Ch'iu, Chou Jen was wont to say, 'Put forth thy strength in the ranks; leave them rather than do wrong.' Who would choose as guide one that is no prop in danger, who cannot lift him when fallen? Moreover, what thou sayest is wrong. If a tiger or a buffalo escape from the pen, if tortoiseshell or jade be broken in the case, who is to blame?"

Jan Yu said: "But Chuan-yümu is strong, and close to Pi;[5] if not seized to-day, it will bring sorrow in after times on our sons and grandsons."

Confucius said: "To make excuses instead of saying 'I want it' is hateful, Ch'iu, to a gentleman. I have heard that unlikeness of lot grieves a king or a chief, not fewness of men. Unrest grieves him, not poverty. Had each his share there would be no poverty. In harmony is number: peace prevents a fall. So if far off tribes will not bend, win them by encouraging worth and learning; and when they come in, give them peace. But now, when far off tribes will not bend, ye two, helpers of your lord, cannot win them. The kingdom is rent asunder; ye are too weak to defend it. Yet spear and shield ye would call up through the land! The sorrows of Chi's grandsons, I fear, will not rise in Chuan-yü: they will rise within the palace wall."

2 Confucius said: "When right prevails below heaven, courtesy, music and punitive wars flow from the Son of

---

[5]A town belonging to the Chi.

Heaven. When wrong prevails below heaven, courtesy, music, and punitive wars flow from the feudal princes. When they flow from the feudal princes they will rarely last for ten generations. When they flow from the princes' ministers they will rarely last for five generations. When courtiers sway a country's fate, they will rarely last for three generations. When right prevails below heaven power does not lie with ministers. When right prevails below heaven common men do not argue."

3 Confucius said: "For five generations its income has passed from the ducal house;[6] for four generations power has lain with ministers: and humbled, therefore, are the sons and grandsons of the three Huan."

4 Confucius said: "There are three friends that do good, and three friends that do harm. The friends that do good are a straight friend, a sincere friend, and a friend who has heard much. The friends that do harm are a smooth friend, a fawning friend, and a friend with a glib tongue."

5 Confucius said: "There are three joys that do good, and three joys that do harm. The joys that do good are joy in dissecting courtesy and music, joy in speaking of the good in men, and joy in a number of worthy friends. The joys that do harm are joy in pomp, joy in roving, and joy in the joys of the feast."

6 Of Lu.

6 Confucius said: "Men who wait upon princes fall into three mistakes. To speak before the time has come is rashness. Not to speak when the time has come is secrecy. To speak heedless of looks is blindness."

7 Confucius said: "A gentleman has three things to guard against. In the days of thy youth, ere they strength is steady, beware of lust. When manhood is reached, in the fulness of strength, beware of strife. In old age, when thy strength is broken, beware of greed."

8 Confucius said: "A gentleman holds three things in awe. He is in awe of Heaven's doom: he is in awe of great men: he is awed by the speech of the holy.

"The vulgar are blind to doom, and hold it not in awe. They are saucy towards the great, and of the speech of the holy they make their game."

9 Confucius said: "The best men are born wise. Next come those who grow wise by learning: then, learned, narrow minds. Narrow minds, without learning, are the lowest of the people."

10 Confucius said: "A gentleman has nine aims. To see clearly; to understand what he hears; to be warm in manner, dignified in bearing, faithful of speech, painstaking at work; to ask when in doubt; in anger to think of difficulties; in sight of gain to remember right."

11 Confucius said: "In sight of good to be filled with longing; to regard evil as scalding to the touch: I have met such men, I have heard such words.

"To dwell apart and search the will; to unriddle truth by righteous life: I have heard these words, but met no such men."

12 Ching, Duke of Ch´i, had a thousand teams of horses; but the people, on his death day, found nought in him to praise. Po-yi[7] and Shu-ch´i starved at the foot of Shouyang, and men to-day still sound their praises.

Is not this the clue to that?

13 Ch´en K´ang[8] asked Po-yü:[9] "Apart from us, have ye heard aught, Sir?"

He answered: "No. Once as I sped across the hall, where my father stood alone, he said to me: 'Dost thou study poetry?' I answered, 'No.' 'Who does not study poetry,' he said, 'has no hold on words.' I withdrew and studied poetry.

"Another day as I sped across the hall, where he stood alone, he said to me: 'Dost thou study courtesy?' I answered, 'No.' 'Who does not study courtesy,' he said, 'loses all foothold.' I withdrew and studied courtesy. These two things I have heard."

[7]See note to 5.22.
[8]The disciple Tzu-ch´in.
[9]Confucius' son.

Ch´en K´ang withdrew and cried gladly: "I asked one thing and get three! I hear of poetry: I hear of courtesy: and I hear, too, that a gentleman keeps aloof from his son."

14 A king speaks of his wife as "my lady." She calls herself "handmaid." Her subjects call her "our royal lady." Speaking to foreigners they say, "our little queen." Foreigners also call her "the royal lady."

1   YANG HUO[1] WISHED to see Confucius. Confucius did not visit him. He sent Confucius a sucking pig. Confucius chose a time when he was out, and went to thank him. They met on the road.

He said to Confucius: "Come, let us speak together. To cherish a gem and undo the kingdom, is that love?"

"It is not," said Confucius.

"To be fond of power and let each chance of office slip, is that wisdom?"

"It is not," said Confucius.

"The days and months glide by; the years do not tarry for us."

"True," said Confucius; "I must take office."

[1]The all-powerful, unscrupulous minister of the Chi.

2 The Master said: "Men are near to each other at birth: the lives they lead sunder them."

3 The Master said: "Only the wisest and the stupidest of men never change."

4 As the Master drew near to Wu-ch'eng[2] he heard sounds of lute and song.

"Why use an ox-knife to kill a fowl?" said the Master, with a pleased smile.

Tzy-yu answered: "Master, I have heard you say of yore: 'A gentleman who has conned the truth will love mankind; poor folk who have conned the truth are easy to rule.'"

"My boys," said the Master, "Yen[3] is right. I spake before in play."

5 Kung-shan Fu-jao[4] held Pi in rebellion. He summoned the Master, who fain would have gone.

Tzu-lu said in displeasure: "This cannot be. Why must ye go to Kung-shan?"

The Master said: "This lord summons me, and would that be all? Could I not make an Eastern Chou[5] of him that employed me?"

---

[2] A very small town, of which the disciple Tzu-yu was governor.
[3] Tzu-yu.
[4] Steward of the Chi and a confederate of Yang Huo.
[5] A kingdom in the east to match Chou in the west, the home of Kings Wen and Wu.

6 Tzu-chang asked Confucius, What is love?

"Love," said Confucius, "is to mete out five things to all below heaven."

"May I ask what they are?"

"Modesty and bounty," said Confucius, "truth, earnestness, and kindness. Modesty escapes insult; bounty wins the many; truth gains men's trust; earnestness brings success; kindness is the key to men's work."

7 Pi Hsi summoned the Master, who fain would have gone.

Tzu-lu said: "Master, I have heard you say of yore: 'When the man in touch with the soul does evil, a gentleman stands aloof.' Pi Hsi holds Chung-mou in rebellion: how, Sir, could ye join him?"

"Yes, I said so," answered the Master. "But is not a thing called hard that cannot be ground thin; white, if steeping will not turn it black? and am I a gourd? can I hang without eating?"

8 The Master said: "Hast thou heard the six words, Yu,[6] or the six they sink into?"

He answered: "No."

"Sit down that I may tell thee. The thirst for love, without love of learning, sinks into fondness. Love of knowledge, without love of learning sinks into presumption. Love of

---

[6]Tzu-lu.

truth, without love of learning sinks into cruelty. Love of uprightness, without love of learning, sinks into harshness. Love of courage, without love of learning, sinks into turbulence. Love of strength, without love of learning, sinks into oddity."

9 The Master said: "My boys, why do ye not study poetry? Poetry would ripen you; teach you insight, fellow-feeling, and forbearance; show you first your duty to your father, then your duty to the king; and would teach you the names of many birds and beasts, plants and trees."

10 The Master said to Po-yü: "Hast thou conned the Chou-nan[8] and Shao-nan?[8] Who has not conned the Chou-nan and Shao-nan is as a man standing with his face to the wall."

11 The Master said: "'Courtesy, courtesy,' is the cry: but are jade and silk the whole of courtesy? 'Harmony, harmony,' is the cry: but are bells and drums the whole of harmony?"

12 The Master said: "A fierce outside and a weak core, is it not like a paltry fellow, like a thief who crawls through a hole in the wall?"

13 The Master said: "The bane of all things noble is the pattern citizen."

---

[7] His son.
[8] The first two books of the "Book of Poetry."

14   The Master said: "To proclaim each truth, as soon as learned to the highwayside, is to lay waste the soul."

15   The Master said: "How can one serve the king with a sordid colleague, itching to get what he wants, trembling to lose what he has? This trembling to lose what he has may lead him anywhere."

16   The Master said: "Men of old had three failings, which have, perhaps, died out to-day. Ambitious men of old were not nice: ambitious men to-day are unprincipled. Masterful men of old were rough: masterful men to-day are quarrelsome. Simple men of old were straight: simple men to-day are false. That is all."

17   The Master said: "Honeyed words and flattering looks seldom speak of love."

18   The Master said: "I hate the ousting of scarlet by purple. I hate the strains of Cheng, confounders of sweet music. I hate a sharp tongue, the ruin of kingdom and home."

19   The Master said: "I long for silence."

Tzu-kung said: "If ye, Sir, were silent, what would your disciples have to tell?"

The Master said: "Does Heaven speak? The seasons four revolve, and all things multiply. Does Heaven speak?"

20 Ju Pei wished to see Confucius. Confucius excused himself on the plea of sickness. As the messenger went out, Confucius took a lute and sang to it, so that he should hear.

21 Tsai Wo[9] asked about the three years' mourning. He thought one enough.

"If for three years pomp is scouted by the gentry, will not courtesy suffer? If music stop for three years, will not music decay? The old grain vanishes, the new springs up; the round of woods for the fire-drill is ended in one year."

The Master said: "Feeding on rice, clad in brocade, couldst thou feel happy?"

"I could feel happy," he answered.

"Then do what makes thee happy. A gentleman, when in mourning, has no taste for sweets, no ear for music; he is unhappy in his home. And so he forsakes these things. But since thou art happy in them, keep them."

When Tsai Wo had left, the Master said: "A man without love! At the age of three a child first leaves his parents' arms, and three years is the time for mourning everywhere below heaven. But did Yü[10] enjoy for three years a father's and a mother's love?"

22 The Master said: "Bad it is when a man eats his fill all day, and has nought to task the mind! Could he not play at chequers? Even that were better."

[9]A disciple.
[10]Tsai Wo.

23 Tzu-lu said: "Does a gentleman honour courage?"

The Master said: "Right comes first for a gentleman. Courage, without sense of right, makes rebels of the great, and robbers of the poor."

24 Tzu-kung said: "Does a gentleman also hate?"

"He does," said the Master. "He hates the sounding of evil deeds; he hates men of low estate who slander their betters; he hates courage without courtesy; he hates daring matched with blindness."

"And Tz´u,[11] he added, "dost thou hate too?"

"I hate those who mistake spying for wisdom. I hate those who take want of deference for courage. I hate evil speaking, cloaked as honesty."

25 The Master said: "Only girls and servants are hard to train. Draw near to them, they grow unruly; hold them off, they pay you with spite."

26 The Master said: "When a man of forty is hated, it will be so to the end."

---

[11]Tzu-kung.

1 THE LORD OF Wei[1] went into exile, the lord of Chi[1] became a slave, Pi-kan[1] died for his reproofs.

Confucius said: "In three of the Yin there was love."

2 When Liu-hsia Hui[2] was judge he was thrice dismissed.

Men said: "Why not leave, Sir?"

He answered: "Whither could I go and not be thrice dismissed for upright service? To do crooked service what need to leave the land of my forefathers?"

3 Ching, Duke of Ch'i, speaking of how to treat Confucius, said: "I could not treat him as I do the Chi. I should set him between Chi and Meng."

[1]Kinsman of Chou, the last tyrannical emperor of the house of Yin.
[2]See note to 15.13.

Again he said: "I am old: I have no use for him."

Confucius went his way.

4 Chi Huan accepted a gift of singing girls from the men of Ch´i.[3] For three days no court was held.

Confucius went his way.

5 Chieh-yü, the mad-head of Ch´u, as he passed Confucius sang:—

> "Phoenix, bright phoenix,
> Thy glory is ended!
> Think of the future:
> The past can't be mended.
> Up and away!
> The court is to-day
> With danger attended."

Confucius alighted and fain would have spoken with him. But hurriedly he made off: no speech was to be had of him.

6 Ch´ang-chü and Chieh-ni were working together in the fields. Confucius, as he passed by, sent Tzu-lu to ask after a ford.

Ch´ang-chü said: "Who is that holding the reins?"

"K´ung Ch´iu,"[4] answered Tzu-lu.

---

[3]B.C. 497. The turning point in Confucius' career. Sorrowfully the Master left office and his native land and went forth to twelve years of wandering in exile.
[4]Confucius.

"What, K´ung Ch´iu of Lu?"

"The same," said Tzu-lu.

"He knows the ford," said Ch´ang-chü.

Tzu-lu asked Chieh-ni.

"Who are ye, sir?" he answered.

"I am Chung Yu."

"The disciple of K´ung Ch´iu of Lu?"

"Yes," said Tzu-lu.

"The world is one seething torrent," answered Chieh-ni, "what man can guide it? Were it not better to choose a master who flees the world, than a master who flees this man and that man?"

And he went on hoeing without stop.

Tzu-lu went back and told the Master, whose face fell.

"Can I herd with birds and beasts?" he said. "Whom but these men can I choose as fellows? And if all were right with the world, I should have no call to set it straight."

7   Tzu-lu having fallen behind met an old man bearing a basket on his staff.

Tzu-lu asked him: "Have ye seen the Master, Sir?"

The old man answered: "Thou dost not toil with thy limbs, nor canst thou tell one grain from another; who is thy Master?"

And planting his staff in the ground, he began weeding.

Tzu-lu bowed and stood before him.

He kept Tzu-lu for the night, killed a fowl, prepared millet, feasted him, and presented his two sons.

On the morrow Tzu-lu went to the Master, and told what had happened.

The Master said: "He is in hiding."

He sent Tzu-lu back to see him; but when he reached the house the man had left.

Tzu-lu said: "Not to take office is wrong. If the ties of old and young are binding, why should the claim of king on minister be set aside? Wishing to keep his person clean, he flouts a foremost duty. A gentleman takes office at the call of right, aware though he be, that the cause is lost."

8 Po-yi, Shu-ch´i, Yü-chung, Yi-yi, Chu-chang, Liu-hsia Hui and Shao-lien were men who fled the world.

The Master said: "Po-yi[5] and Shu-ch´i would not bend the will, or shame the body.

"We can but say that Liu-hsia Hui[6] and Shao-lien bent the will and shamed the body. Their words jumped with duty; their deeds answered our hopes.

[5]See note to 5.22.
[6]See note to 15.13.

"We may say of Yü-chung and Yi-yi that they lived in hiding, but gave the rein to the tongue. They were clean in person: their retreat was timely.

"But I am unlike all of these: I know not 'must' or 'must not.'"

9 Chih, the chief Musical Conductor, went to Ch´i; Kan, the Conductor at the second meal, went to Ch´u; Liao, the Conductor at the third meal, went to Ts´ai; Chü-eh, the Conductor at the fourth meal, went to Ch´in. The drum master Fang-shu crossed the river; the tambourine master Wu crossed the Han; Yang, the assistant Bandmaster, and Hsiang, who played the sounding stones, crossed the sea.

10 The Duke of Chou[7] said to the Duke of Lu:[8] "A prince does not forsake kinsmen, nor offend great vassals by neglect. He will not discard an old servant, unless he have big cause. He asks perfection of no man."

11 Chou had eight officers: Po-ta and Po-kuo, Chung-tu and Chung-hu, Shu-yeh and Shu-hsia, Chi-sui and Chi-kua.

[7]See note to 7.5.
[8]His son.

19

1   TZU-CHANG SAID: "The scholar who in danger will stake his life, who in sight of gain remembers right, who is lowly in heart at worship, and sad at heart when mourning, may pass muster."

2   Tzu-chang said: "Goodness blindly clutched, faith that lacks simplicity, can they be said to be, or said not to be?"

3   The disciples of Tzu-hsia asked Tzu-chang about friendship.

Tzu-chang said: "What does Tzu-hsia say?"

They answered: "Tzu-hsia says: 'Cling to worthy friends; push the unworthy away.'"

Tzu-chang said: "I was taught otherwise. A gentleman honours worth, and bears with the many. He applauds goodness, and pities weakness. Am I a man of great worth, what could I not bear with in men? Am I a man without worth, men will push me away. Why should I push others away?"

4 Tzu-hsia said: "Though there is no trade without interest, a gentleman will not follow one, lest it clog the mind at length."

5 Tzu-hsia said: "Who recalls each day what fails him, who each month forgets nothing won, he may indeed be called fond of learning!"

6 Tzu-hsia said: "Through wide learning and singleness of aim, through keen questions and searchings of heart we come to love."

7 Tzu-hsia said: "To learn their trade apprentices work in a shop: by study a gentleman reaches to truth."

8 Tzu-hsia said: "The vulgar always gloss their faults."

9 Tzu-hsia said: "A gentleman alters thrice. Seen from afar he looks stern: as we draw near, he thaws: but the sound of his words is sharp."

10 Tzu-hsia said: "A gentleman lays no burdens on the people until they have learned to trust him. Unless they trusted him they would think him cruel. Until he is trusted he does not reprove. Unless he were trusted it would seem fault-finding."

11 Tzu-hsia said: "If we keep within the bounds of honour, we may step to and fro through propriety."

12 Tzu-yu said: "The disciples, the boys of Tzu-hsia, can sprinkle and sweep the floor, answer when spoken to, and enter or leave a room; but what can come of branches without root?"

When Tzu-hsia heard this, he said: "Yen Yu[1] is wrong. In training a gentleman, because we teach one thing first, shall we flag before reaching the next? Thus plants and trees vary in size. Should a gentleman's training bewilder him? To absorb it first and last none but the holy are fit."

13 Tzu-hsia said: "Crown servants should use their spare strength for study. A scholar with his spare strength should serve the crown."

14 Tzu-yu said: "Mourning should stretch to grief, and stretch no further."

15 Tzu-yu said: "My friend Chang[2] can do things that are hard, but he is void of love."

16 Tseng-tzu said: "So magnificent is Chang that to do as love bids is hard when at his side."

[1]Tzu-yu.
[2]Tzu-chang.

17 Tseng-tzu said: "I have heard the Master say: 'Man never shows what is in him unless when mourning one near to him.'"

18 Tseng-tzu said: "I have heard the Master say: 'In all else we may rival the piety of Meng Chuang, but in not changing his father's ministers, or his father's rule, he is hard to rival.'"

19 The Meng[3] made Yang Fu[4] criminal judge, who asked Tseng-tzu about his duties.

Tseng-tzu said: "The gentry have lost their way, and the people long been distraught. When thou dost get at the heart of a crime, be moved to pity, not puffed with joy."

20 Tzu-kung said: "The wickedness of Chou[5] was not so great. Thus let princes beware of living in a sink, where the filth of the world all streams together!"

21   Tzu-kung said: "The faults of a prince are like the darkening of sun or moon. The fault is seen of all, and when he breaks free all men admire."

22 Kung-sun Ch´ao of Wei asked Tzu-kung: "Where did Chung-ni[6] get his learning?"

---

[3]The chief of the Meng clan, powerful in Lu.
[4]A disciple of Tseng-tzu.
[5]The foul tyrant, last of the house of Yin.
[6]Confucius.

Tzu-kung said: "The lore of Wen and Wu has not fallen into ruin, but lives in men: the big in big men, the small in small men. No man is empty of the lore of Wen and Wu. How should the Master not learn it? What need had he for a set teacher?"

23 Shu-sun Wu-shu,[7] talking to some lords at court, said: "Tzu-kung is a greater man than Chung-ni"[8]

Tzu-fu Ching-po told this to Tzu-kung.

Tzu-kung said: "This is like the palace and its wall. My wall reaches to the shoulder. Peeping over one sees the goodly home within. The Master's wall is many fathoms high. Unless he enter the gate, no man can see the beauty of the Ancestral Temples, the wealth of the hundred officers. And if but few men gain the gate, is my lord not right to speak as he does?"

24 Shu-sun Wu-shu decried Chung-ni.

Tzu-kung said: "It is labour lost. Chung-ni cannot be cried down. The greatness of other men is a mound that can be overleaped. Chung-ni is the sun or moon that no man can overleap. To run into death though a man were ready, how could he hurt the sun or moon? His want of sense would but show the better!"

[7] Head of the Meng clan.
[8] Confucius.

131

25 Ch´en Tzu-ch´in[9] said to Tzu-kung: "Sir, your humility is overdone. In what way is Chung-ni your better?

Tzu-kung said: "By a word a gentleman betrays wisdom, by a word his want of wisdom. Words are not to be lightly spoken. None can come up to the Master, as heaven is not to be climbed by steps. Had the Master power in the land, the saying would come true: 'All that he plants takes root; whither he leads men follow. The peace he brings draws men; his touch tunes them to harmony: honored in life, he is mourned when dead.' Who can come up to him?"

9The disciple Tzu-ch´in.

1 [1]YAO SAID: "Hail to thee, Shun! The number that the Heavens are telling falls on thee. Keep true hold of the golden mean. Should there be stress or want within the four seas, the gift of Heaven will pass for ever."

Shun laid the same commands on Yü.

T'ang said: "I, Thy child Li, make bold to offer this black steer, and make bold to proclaim before Thee, Almighty Lord, that I dare not forgive sin, nor hold down Thy servants. Search them, oh Lord, in Thine heart. Visit not my sins on the ten thousand hamlets: the sins of the ten thousand hamlets visit upon my head."

Chou bestowed great gifts, and good men grew rich.

[1]This chapter shows the principles on which China was governed in ancient days. Yao and Shun were the legendary founders of the Chinese Empire. Yü, T'ang, and Chou were the first emperors of the houses of Hsia, Shang, and Chou, which had ruled China up to the time of Confucius.

"Loving hearts are better than men that are near of kin. All the people throw the blame upon me alone."[2]

He attended to weights and measures, revised the laws, and restored broken officers. On all sides order reigned. He revived states that had perished, and gave back fiefs that had reverted. He called forth men from hiding. All hearts below heaven turned to him. The people's food, burials, and worship he held to be of moment. His bounty gained the many; his truth won the people's trust; his earnestness brought success; his justice made men glad.

2 Tzu-chang asked Confucius: "How should men be governed?"

The Master said: "He who would govern men must honour the five graces, spurn the four vices."

Tzu-chang said: "What are the five graces?"

The Master said: "A gentleman is kind, but not wasteful; he burdens, but does not embitter; he is covetous, not sordid; high-minded, not proud; he inspires awe, and not fear."

Tzu-chang said: "What is meant by kindness without waste?"

The Master said: "To further what furthers the people, is not that kindness without waste? If burdens be sorted to strength, who will grumble? To covet love and win love,

---

[2]Said by King Wu (Chou). The people blamed him for not dethroning at once the infamous tyrant Chou Hsin.

is that sordid? Few or many, small or great, all is one to a gentleman: he dare not slight any man. Is not this to be high-minded and not proud? A gentleman straightens his robe and settles his face. He is stern, and men look up to him with dread. Is not this to inspire awe, and not fear?"

Tzu-chang said: "What are the four vices?"

The Master said: "To leave untaught and then kill is cruelty: to ask full tale without warning is tyranny: to give careless orders, and be strict when the day comes is robbery: to be stingy in rewarding men is littleness."

3 The Master said: "A man who is blind to doom can be no gentleman. Without a knowledge of courtesy we must want foothold. Without a knowledge of words there is no understanding men."